Th ⊃ Book

* *

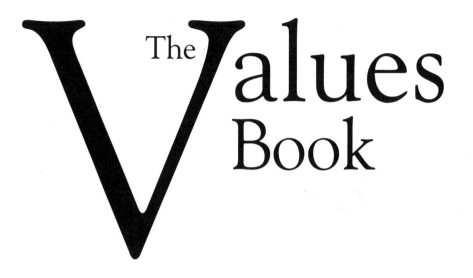

The Values Book

Teaching 16 Basic Values to Young Children

Pam Schiller and Tamera Bryant
Illustrations by Cheryl Kirk Noll

gryphon house

Beltsville, Maryland

Dedication

To Rose and Samuel Marotta Sr., mother and father of Samuel
Marotta Jr., whose sense of values I hold in highest esteem.
PS

To my A-list
Ashley, who taught me the meaning of loyalty and compassion.
Austin, who renewed my sense of wonder and joy.
Alyssa, who restored my faith.
Aunt Delsie, who has forever shown me the value of humor,
self-reliance and resourcefulness.
TB

Copyright © 1998 Pam Schiller and Tamera Bryant

Published by Gryphon House, Inc.
10726 Tucker Street, Beltsville, MD 20705

World Wide Web: http://www.ghbooks. com

Library of Congress Cataloging-in-Publication Data

Schiller, Pam Byrne.
    The values book : teaching 16 basic values to young children / Pam
  Schiller and Tamera Bryant : illustrations by Cheryl Kirk Noll.
        P. cm.
    Includes index.
    ISBN 0-87659-189-6
    1. Child rearing.   2. Children--Conduct of life.   3. Social
  values--Study and teaching.   4. Parent and child.   5. Creative
  activities and seatwork.   I. Bryant, Tamera, 1955-   II. Title.
  HV769.S285   1998
  649'. 1--DC21   98-13680
                                                                CIP

The Values Book

Table of Contents

Introduction

American society is changing rapidly. Technology, our socioeconomic structure, our family structure and our business culture are just a few of the areas that have changed dramatically over the past twenty years. Each of those changes has created, and continues to create, its own ripple effect in our attitudes and behaviors. For example, as we are able to obtain things we want or need quickly, whether it be a microwaveable hot dog, instant credit or information through the Internet, we become less patient and less resourceful. We're not called on to practice those values. We hear of families separating at the first hint of adversity. What has happened to commitment? When companies downsize and force workers to change jobs, what happens to loyalty?

The truth is that in our hurry-up society, we don't always stop to think of all the consequences of the cultural changes taking place. We need to look forward, considering the effects of our actions. It's time that we question our own value system. Are we willing to let go of patience, commitment, loyalty and the other values we've traditionally held? If so, how will we replace them? If not, how will we instill these values in our children? What strategies will we use to replace the societal structures that upheld those values?

Looking at history, we see that it was patience, commitment, loyalty and independence that resulted in the cure for polio, the moon landing, the perfection of the heart transplant, the electric light, penicillin and the telephone. It is time to decide what values are important to the future of our children and families and then to support and encourage the practice of those values in our daily lives. Whose responsibility is it to teach values to our children? The responsibility belongs to each of us. Whether we realize it or not, we are always teaching values, but we must put more conscious effort into that teaching. The values we impart to

The Values Book

our children today, consciously and unconsciously, will have a major impact on society tomorrow. If we continue to leave the teaching of values mostly to chance, we, as a nation, risk losing an integral piece of our culture altogether.

Using This Book

The Values Book focuses on finding new ways to instill traditional values. Citing circumstances within our culture and environment that are creating changes in our behaviors, this book offers teachers and parents quick and straightforward methods for raising children's awareness, understanding and practical experience of basic values. How each of us ranks these values in terms of importance may vary, and it is possible that some readers will choose to maintain a particular value and others to let it go. We challenge you to determine which values are important to you, and we encourage you to begin focusing on modeling, teaching and practicing them with the children in your care.

The chapters in this book follow an easy-to-use format, addressing specific values through definition, ideas for thought and discussion and suggestions for activities and books that reinforce values. Each chapter is filled with concrete, easy-to-do activities and projects that foster the development of values in children. Because we believe that children also learn through observing and imitating adults, the book is packed with ideas and suggestions for using modeling as an important strategy.

Chapter Introduction: A Poem or Song and a Definition

Each chapter begins with a quote from a children's song or poem that reflects the essence of the message in that chapter. A definition/description of the value being presented is provided for clarity and to establish a common ground.

Why Is This Value Important? Things for Adults to Think About

This section presents a series of thought-provoking statements for **adults**. These statements are intended to help you understand how societal influences might affect and alter opportunities for developing a value.

Included are several open-ended questions to help you reflect on your own understanding and feelings regarding the value in question. These questions are perfect for helping focus a discussion about values during staff development sessions, retreats, in-service training and parent meetings.

Talking With Children About Values

In this section the focus changes to children. Simple questions and statements that are meaningful to children are provided to develop their understanding of the intellectual and emotional aspects of the value. These questions can be used anytime during the day to engage children in discussion. They are particularly effective during circle or group time and snack or lunch time.

Things to Do in the Classroom

Again focusing on children, this section contains a collection of activities for teachers to implement at school. Activities for individual children as well as for small and large groups of children are included. Each activity provides opportunities for children to practice behaviors that lead to the forming of a specific value. Some activities support more than one value; therefore, they may overlap.

Working With Families: Ideas for Home

Continuity between home and school is important, so this section of each chapter is filled with activities and ideas for parents to use at home as an extension and reinforcement of the child's classroom values learning experiences.

Books to Share With Children

Each chapter concludes with a bibliography of children's books that support the value discussed in that chapter. The book list is intended for use by both teachers and parents.

Compassion & Empathy

In a cabin in a wood
Little man by his window stood,
Saw a rabbit hopping by
Knocking at his door.

"Help me! Help me! Help me!" he said.
"I need a place to rest my head."
"Little rabbit, come inside
Safely to abide."

Compassion & Empathy

What Are Compassion and Empathy?

As we acknowledge other people's

feelings, thoughts and experiences,

we naturally feel compassion for

them—a personal identification with

them and a desire to help them in

any distress. Through empathy

we recognize our own humanity

in others.

Why Are Compassion and Empathy Important? Things for Adults to Think About

■ Compassion and empathy begin to develop in the very first years of life. Most scientists assume that we are biologically wired for these feelings, but we must recognize and nurture this natural inclination toward caring.

Have you ever told a young child that your head hurts or that you've had a really bad day? Have children seen you cry? What happened? Do you agree that young children are naturally compassionate? How can we encourage this? How do we discourage it?

■ Compassion and empathy encompass respect for all living things, even the tiniest of creatures that have no voice to speak for themselves.

Is it okay to step on a snail? How is stepping on a snail different from pulling a dog's tail? How is pulling a dog's tail different from hitting someone?

■ Television and movie violence are being blamed for creating an apathetic attitude about helping others within society. Children and adults are becoming jaded to scenes of violence that were at one time both shocking and sickening. As violence permeates our society, is our capacity for compassion diminishing?

Watch television for several hours over a few days, and record the number of violent acts you see. Can you remember when violence had a more profound effect on you? Can you remember when graphic violence was not allowed on television? How do you feel about watching news reports of real violence, including war scenes, on television? Are your feelings different when the violence is real?

Talking With Children About Compassion and Empathy

Are compassion and empathy values worth keeping? Talk with children about the ideas below and see what they think.

■ What does it mean to be kind to a friend? How does it feel when a friend is kind to you? What does it mean to be kind to animals?

■ Think about a time when someone hurt you. What happened? How did you feel?

■ With young children, say the Little Rabbit poem, making up hand motions to go along. Ask the children to describe how the rabbit feels. Why is he tired? Has he been running from a fox? Did something frighten him? The man understands how the little rabbit feels and wants to help him. Discuss the man's kindness.

■ What do you think happens when you step on a worm or a bug? Do you realize that the worm will never eat again? Never crawl again? That its life is over? Everything has a job to do. If you kill it, it can't do its job.

■ Brainstorm a list of all the things you need to do to take good care of a pet.

■ Think of a time when you were hurt or sick. Who took care of you? How did that person take care of you? Have you helped take care of someone? Have you helped someone to feel better?

Develop children's language skills and continue your discussion of compassion and empathy by weaving the following vocabulary words into your day.

caring	helping
compassion	kindness
empathy	thoughts
experiences	feelings

Things to Do in the Classroom

Activities for children of all ages

■ Avoid singing songs that show no compassion, such as "Baby Bumble Bee" and "Little Bunny Foo Foo." If you do sing these songs, use them to initiate a conversation about the feelings of others.

■ Instead of using a long list of rules, try using just one—"I can freely explore my classroom as long as I do nothing that hurts myself or others." It is amazing how this one rule covers everything and how often it focuses on feelings.

■ Make a set of feeling faces by drawing features on plates and attaching them to tongue depressors. At least twice a week, pose scenarios that require children to think about their feelings and the feelings of others. Relate them to actual events in the classroom when possible. For example, if Tiffany and Richele were arguing over a toy, pose a scenario where two children (with different names) are fighting over a toy. When the children determine which feeling the scenario evokes, they can hold up the corresponding plate. Ask a few children to explain their choices. Compassion and empathy are based on an understanding of feelings, first your own, then an ability to transfer that understanding to others.

■ Get a pet for the classroom and involve everyone in caring for it.

■ Take the children on nature hikes. Point out as many small creatures as you can find and discuss how each one fits into the ecosystem.

■ Model compassion when disciplining children. Respect their privacy. Make sure you are calm before you jump in to "handle" a situation.

■ Visit a senior citizen home. Encourage the children to plan a program or take artwork to share. Be sure children have opportunities to interact with residents. When you come back to school, talk about the trip. How many smiles did the children create during their visit? How do they feel about those smiles?

■ Set up a doctor's office or veterinary clinic in the Dramatic Play center. Visit a real clinic if you can.

Activities for older children

■ When children hurt others or get into squabbles with their friends, help them identify how their words and actions affect others. Assist them in becoming peace-makers. Teach the following process: children sit down and listen to each other's side, each one makes suggestions for compromise, then a suggestion is selected and tried. The process continues until children feel satisfied, or at least better.

■ Put on a carnival for other classrooms or schools and give the proceeds to a charitable cause. Invite children to work together to decide how they will donate the money. You might take a field trip to let the children make their donation in person. Let children see where and how their money is used.

■ Appoint a Compassion Crew (two or three children). Make a Compassion Button for each member. Ask the crew to watch their classmates. When crew members see someone being kind or compassionate, they give a button to that person. The new button-wearers find other compassionate children and continue to pass the buttons on.

■ Encourage the children to try telling a story from another point of view, for example, that of the classroom pet (bunny, hamster, etc.). How would the pet like you to take care of it? What does it feel like to be the pet? What does the pet add to your classroom?

Working With Families: Ideas for Home

Activities for children of all ages

■ Model respect for all living things. Collect harmless insects that get inside the house and let them loose outside. Avoid purposely stepping on insects. Pick only the number of flowers you really need or the amount of fruit you will really use.

■ Use compassion when disciplining. Remember, everyone deserves a warning, and we all make mistakes. Use a kind and tempered voice and be sure the punishment fits the crime.

■ Discuss your feelings of compassion with your children. If you are saddened by

something on the news, share those feelings.

■ Use television programs as discussion points for understanding and respecting the feelings of others. Children's television programming is filled with examples—positive and negative.

■ Encourage your children to help you gather items for Goodwill Industries or other charitable organizations.

■ Keep stick-on stars. When someone in the family does something nice for another family member, let her wear a star.

Activities for older children

■ Take your children to work in a food kitchen or homeless shelter. If your fire department has a toy drive, encourage your children to make a donation.

■ "Adopt" a child. Many hospitals, shelters and foster care agencies organize programs for needy children.

■ If you have more than one child, talk with them about their birth order. How does it feel to be the oldest? What's the best thing? The worst thing? How do you feel about your brothers and sisters? If your child is an only child, ask how that feels.

Books to Share With Children

Read books that illustrate and encourage compassion and empathy. Check your library for some of those listed here. Each one provides opportunities to discuss the results of being sensitive to the feelings of others.

Alexander and the Terrible, Horrible, No Good, Very Bad Day by Judith Viorst
Alfie Gives a Hand by Shirley Hughes
Amazing Grace by Mary Hoffman
Dancing With the Indians by Angela Shelf Medearis
Feelings by Aliki
Going Home by Eve Bunting
Gracias, Rosa by Michelle Markel
Heart to Heart by George Shannon
I Can Hear the Sun by Patricia Polacco
Our Wish by Ralph da Costa Nunez
The Tie Man's Miracle by Steven Schnur
Uncle Willie and the Soup Kitchen by Dyanne DiSalvo-Ryan

·*·*·*·* The Values Book

Cooperation

The more we get together, together, together,
The more we get together, the happier we'll be.

 Cooperation

What Is Cooperation?

Combining our energies to work

with others toward a common goal

is cooperation. Through coopera-

tion we can accomplish tasks

more quickly and easily than by

ourselves, with the added benefit

of enjoying each other's company

as we share in the work.

Why Is Cooperation Important?
Things for Adults to Think About

■ American society was built on the concept of cooperation. The Pilgrims could not have survived had they not combined their talents and resources for the good of the whole. Their challenges were numerous. It took the thinking, reasoning and talents of many to survive. They sought independence from England, not from humankind.

Who helped the Pilgrims learn basic survival skills?

■ Early pioneers traveled across the country in groups for the same reason. Communities were established by combining resources. Barn raisings, quilting bees and the barter system were all outcomes of a society that recognized strength in numbers. Most people today don't build their own homes or make their own bed covers. We buy them ready made.

What other early American practices can you think of that required a cooperative effort?

■ Until recently, neighborhoods were more interdependent. People needed each other. They socialized, formed carpools and watched over each other's children and homes.

When was the last time a neighbor asked you for help? When was the last time you asked a neighbor for help?

■ As we've moved from an agrarian to an industrial to an electronic business culture, the way we interact with each other has also changed. We've moved from working side by side on assembly lines to telecommuting, working in isolation from our colleagues.

Does this mean that we don't need each other? Is cooperation easier now or more difficult?

■ Technology has given us wings, but it is dichotomous. As it frees us to be independent, it binds us to an even larger number of people. We are becoming a global community—connected to and interdependent with a diverse new group of people.

Brainstorm a list of technology that connects the far corners of the world.

■ We get the best results through the efforts of many. We need combined personality types, talents and knowledge bases to be most productive. Humans need interactions with other humans. Through cooperation we learn to compromise, negotiate and share.

Think about the last time you worked on a group project. What did you learn?

Talking With Children About Cooperation

Is cooperation a value worth keeping? Talk with children about the questions below and see what they think.

■ What things do you and your friends do together? What games are more fun when you play them with friends?

■ With young children, sing "The More We Get Together." Talk about the many things children do together in the classroom or in partnership with family members at home. Point out the differences in doing things alone and in working as a part of a group effort.

■ What jobs do you have at home or school that someone helps you with?

■ Think of a job that each member of your family does at home. What would happen if one person had to do all the jobs? Could one person do all the jobs?

■ Brainstorm a list of things that you can't do by yourself.

Develop children's language skills and continue your discussion of cooperation by weaving the following vocabulary words into your day.

companionship	help
compromise	partnership
cooperation	share
efforts	teamwork
friends	together

The Values Book

Things to Do in the Classroom

Activities for children of all ages

■ Paint a mural. Hang it up and label it with all the artists' names.

■ Play cooperative games:

TUG OF PEACE—Tie the ends of a long piece of rope, 12" to 18" (30cm-45cm) per child, to make a circle. Lay it on the floor and invite the children to sit around the outside. Challenge the children to grab the rope and pull themselves to a standing position. You may want to practice in small groups then move to the full group.

PRETZEL PASS—Invite the children to stand or sit in a circle. Give each child a chopstick, straw or dowel rod. Place a large pretzel on every other stick. Challenge the children to pass the pretzels around the circle using only their chopsticks. You can use any circular snack for this activity.

Cooperation

COIN COVER-UP—Put about 8″ (20 cm) of water in a plastic tub or bucket. Place a quarter on the bottom in the center. Give children a penny each. Invite them to drop their pennies in the water one at a time. The object is to completely cover the quarter with the pennies.

■ Play games with no winners and no losers:

COOPERATIVE MUSICAL CHAIRS—Set up chairs as you would for a regular game of musical chairs. Start with one chair for each child. After one round of the game, remove one or two chairs. Here's where the game is different. The next time the music stops, the children must figure a way for everyone to have a seat even though there are not enough chairs. For example, they may share chairs, push chairs together to make a bigger chair, or sit in each other's laps. Continue to remove chairs each time the music stops. Continue the game as long as there is a seat for everyone when the music stops.

BACK-TO-BACK LIFTS—Invite children to choose partners. Ask partners to sit back to back on the floor. On the count of three, partners help each other stand, keeping their backs together and pushing against each other.

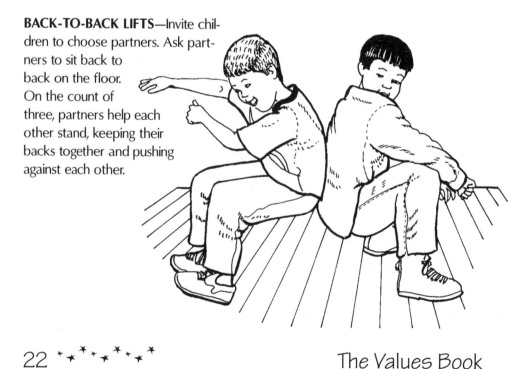

THREE-LEGGED MOVEMENT—Invite children to choose partners and stand side by side. Use wide, soft cloths to tie inside legs together. Invite partners to walk, skip, skate, crawl or run. They can't do it without working together. You can try variations of this game by tying elbows or hands together and having partners try to paint, clean up, wash dishes or do other classroom activities together.

LARGE BALL RELAY—Divide the class into groups of four or five. Give each group a large ball. Mark Start and Finish lines on the floor with tape. The object of the game is for each team member to move the team's ball from Start to Finish and back. The trick is that no two team members can move the ball in the same way. Encourage teams to decide how each member will move the ball (carry, kick, bounce, hold on head, etc.), then let them go.

■ Raise money for charitable activities:

Have a sidewalk art sale. Let each child create a painting and then sell it for a donation. Framing the paintings may increase their likelihood of being sold. You might also contact a local bank or Chamber of Commerce about displaying and selling the artwork.

Put on a carnival. Let children plan booths and make props. Invite the neighborhood to participate. Sell tickets and donate the proceeds to a charity.

■ Read *Stone Soup* by Marcia Brown, then make stone soup with the children. (See page 42 for a soup recipe.) It's a great experience in cooperative effort. Encourage each child to participate in some way—chopping celery, measuring, pouring in the carrots, stirring and so on.

■ Display pictures of people working and playing together. Discuss the activities in the pictures.

■ Invite a group of senior citizens to assist with and participate in classroom activities. This type of interaction encourages children to network and cooperate with diverse groups.

■ Ask a group of older children to come to your classroom and teach your children something. Tying shoes is a great lesson.

■ Have a group work project, such as caring for a class pet, cleaning up a specific area of the room or taking care of a garden.

■ Go on a litter walk. Clean up around the school grounds or neighborhood.

Activities for older children

■ Put on a play. It takes a lot of cooperative effort to make props, costumes and backdrops. Invite children from other classrooms or parents to be the audience.

■ Plan an exchange project with another school. This could be a pen pal (or picture pal) arrangement, a joint puppet show or even joint participation in the carnival or art show described above.

Working With Families: Ideas for Home

Activities for children of all ages

■ Plant a family garden of flowers, herbs or vegetables. Decide together what each person will be responsible for (planting, watering, weeding, cutting or picking). Share as many jobs as possible. Talk often about how the garden is growing, how it belongs to everyone and how it takes everyone to share the work of caring for the garden.

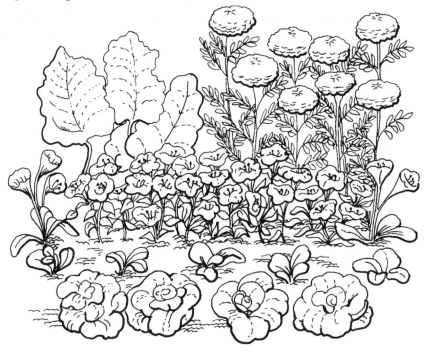

The Values Book

■ Make a recipe together. Invite your child to help pour, cut, chop, stir, serve and so on. (See pages 42, 43, 101 and 102 for recipes to try.)

■ Play Cooperative Hide and Seek. This requires the whole family and maybe even some friends to join in. Choose one person to be IT. Instead of IT looking for others, IT hides and the others go looking for IT. IT should hide in a place that is large enough for the group to fit in, because as each participant finds IT, they join in the hiding place. Continue until everyone is hiding together.

■ Create a chart that shows chores that must be done to keep the household running smoothly. As a group, assign each chore to a family member or family team. Use stickers or markers to show the completion of each chore. Rotate jobs each week or each month so that family members gain an appreciation for the variety of chores.

■ Participate in a neighborhood co-op. Perhaps you want to share bulk food purchases or maybe baby-sitting. Whatever the arrangement, this is a good model for children.

Books to Share With Children

Read books that illustrate and encourage cooperation. Check your library for some of those listed here. Each one provides opportunities to talk about people working together.

A Chair for My Mother by Vera Williams
Come Sit by Me by Margaret Merrifield
The Earth and I by Frank Asch
The Listening Walk by Paul Showers
Music, Music for Everyone by Vera Williams
Pookins Gets Her Way by Helen Lester
The Rainbow Fish by Marcus Pfister
Stone Soup by Marsha Brown
Swimmy by Leo Lionni
Together by George Ella Lyon
When the Teddy Bears Came by Martin Waddell

Courage

Little Miss Muffet sat on a tuffet
Eating her curds and whey.
Along came a spider
Who sat down beside her
And frightened Miss Muffet away.

Little Miss Muffet went back to her tuffet,
Looked the thing square in the eye.
"See here, you big spider,
Miss Muffet's a fighter.
And you're the one saying bye-bye."

Courage

What Is Courage?

Courage enables us to face difficulty, danger or pain in a way that allows us to maintain control over the situation. We can build courage by identifying things that frighten or challenge us and thinking of strategies for coping with them.

Why Is Courage Important? Things for Adults to Think About

■ When life was simpler, we had fewer immediate things to be fearful of. People developed strategies for coping with fear. Today, many children are afraid to walk outside their homes, to go to school, to stand up to peer pressure. Ours is a violent society. Challenges are big and may appear insurmountable. Children are unable to slowly build strategies for being courageous.

Listen to the evening news. Make a list of the reports involving children and violence.

■ Many people enjoy the adrenaline rush created by fear. We continue to escalate the level of intensity in order to satisfy our need for excitement. Think about horror movies from the 1930s and those made today. How far can we go?

Make a list of ways our society exploits our fears. How do you think this affects our attitudes toward fear and children's ability to build coping strategies?

■ All human beings experience fear. The question is, how do we face it? Fear can immobilize us, or it can motivate us. Our imagination can exaggerate the fear, allowing it to control us, or our mind can help control the fear.

Think of a time you were fearful. How did you react? Did you calm your mind before you acted? What was the outcome of the situation? Did you learn anything about yourself from the experience? About the cause of your fear?

■ Fear is often at the base of many of our actions and reactions. Take envy, for example. Is it really the fear of not being good enough or having enough? What about anger? Is it generated by a fear of loss?

Think about an angry or envious situation you witnessed. Can you trace the feelings to fear? If so, can you see how important it is to summon the courage to overcome fear?

■ Up until the 1950s, people generally raised their children the same way they were raised—as miniature adults. Two situations perpetuated this practice—a lack

of understanding of how children grow and develop and a shortened childhood resulting from chores and responsibilities beginning at a young age.

Following World War II, the United States began a new era of prosperity, and families were able to provide more for their children than they themselves had as children. Encompassed in this new ability to provide for children came the notion of protecting and shielding them. Children were allowed to experience the innocence of childhood for the first time.

But protecting and shielding children from fear can be a disservice. When children experience child-sized fears, they gradually build strategies for coping with those fears. Childhood fears are a normal part of development.

> *Think of some of the things that frightened you when you were a child. What strategies did you use to face your fears then? What fears do you have now? What coping strategies do you use now?*

■ Self-protection programs such as "Beware of Strangers" and "WHO (Good Touch, Bad Touch)" can have adverse effects on children if they are introduced before children can assimilate the information being provided.

> *Have you ever tried to help a three year-old understand the concept of a stranger? Chances are you either got nowhere or you ended up making the child afraid of everyone. Very young children are not capable of generalizing information from one situation to another.*

Talking With Children About Courage

Is courage a value worth keeping? Talk with children about the ideas below and see what they think.

■ Think of a time when you were afraid. What were you afraid of? What did you do? Will you be afraid next time?

■ Do you think big people are ever afraid? Ask big people around you to describe a time when they were afraid. What did they do?

■ With young children, say the Little Miss Muffet poem, then choose a few volunteers to act it out. Talk about the difference in Miss Muffet's reaction to the spider in the two verses. Courage allows Miss Muffet to confront the spider.

The Values Book

Encourage the children to speculate on why Miss Muffet decided to return to her tuffet and how she may have found the courage to face her fear.

■ Is fear ever a good thing? Does it keep us safe sometimes? Can you think of a fear that turned out to be a good thing?

■ Think of strategies for facing fear, like whistling or drawing a picture of what frightens you. How many strategies can you think of?

Develop children's language skills and continue the discussion of courage by weaving the following vocabulary words into your day.

afraid	coping
brave	danger
challenge	fear
courage	imagination
control	strategy

Things to Do in the Classroom

Activities for children of all ages

■ Encourage children to talk about their fears. Many times verbalizing is all that is needed to put fears to rest. Try to help children identify the differences between real and imagined fears.

■ Provide play opportunities that allow children to express their fears. Many children find puppets are a great tool for expressing their feelings.

Courage

■ Dramatize (role play) stories that have a theme of fear in them. Let children create new and different strategies for facing whatever is the cause of the fear. For example, in "The Three Little Pigs," the first and second little pigs run to the third little pig's house when they are afraid. What else could they have done? The billy goats in "The Three Billy Goats Gruff" pass the troll on to their bigger brother. What else could they have done?

■ Call attention to acts of courage that occur in the classroom, in literature and in television news stories (those that children can relate to). Discuss the source of the fear and the actions taken by the people who were afraid.

■ Be aware of children's abilities and limitations so that you can challenge them individually. If Estrella is climbing on the jungle gym and you know she can go higher, encourage her exploration. If Ashley is struggling to make the second level, help him gain confidence before he climbs higher. Remember that confidence is part of courage.

■ Knowledge helps reduce fear by increasing understanding. If Tamika is afraid of bugs, introduce a lesson or a unit on bugs. If Li is afraid of shadows, teach a lesson on shadows.

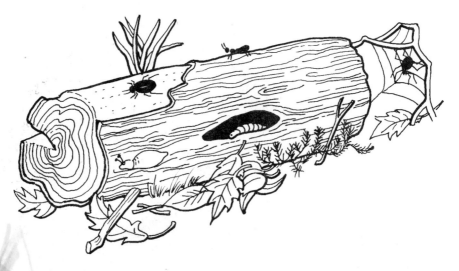

■ To withstand teasing and to stand up to peer pressure, children need courage. A strong sense of self will allow them to see the humor in a situation, to walk away or to ignore the teaser or the tempter. Focus on lessons that promote self-esteem, such as discussing respect for individual differences, exploring and validating feelings and practicing problem-solving and making good choices. You may want to remind children that they can't control others but they can control their reaction to others.

Working With Families: Ideas for Home

Activities for children of all ages

■ Model courage. Let your children see you try a challenging new physical activity like wall climbing or skiing. Or try something less physical like speaking up for something you believe in. Children pick up many of their fears from us, and they also pick up how we handle our fears.

■ Be honest with your children. When you are afraid, tell them, but don't frighten them. Be sure to tell them what you are doing to be less afraid. Choose a fear you would like to overcome, like fear of flying or fear of heights, and take steps to conquer it.

■ Call attention to acts of bravery, those that happen in your family and in the neighborhood.

■ Don't make fun of children's fears. Adults often think creating a joke will diminish the fear, but it usually only imbeds it. Children's imagined fears can seem silly to adults, but to children they are as real as any adult fear.

■ When children express a fear, help them think of ways to be brave. For example, if Sam is afraid of thunder, he might find an adult to be with until the storm is over or play music to drown out the noise. Here's a list of some typical childhood fears, along with strategies for helping children face them.

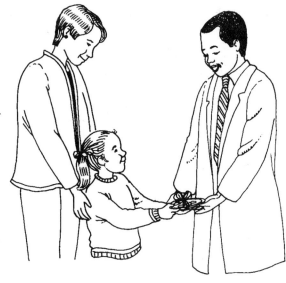

Separation—Leave one of your belongings with your child as reassurance of your return.

Santa Claus—Wait. Don't force or push your child to approach Santa.

Doctors and dentists—Go for a friendly visit first to let your child get acquainted. Bake cookies for the doctor.

Courage

■ When you see that children have specific fears which knowledge will help reduce, offer that knowledge. For example, if Jamie is afraid of water, enroll him in swimming lessons. If Karah is frightened by the sound of the air conditioner starting, show her the compressor and let her see that it cannot harm her.

■ Sometimes children are afraid of things that are difficult or impossible to explain. For example, explaining that cold and hot air colliding creates thunder may mean little to a young child. And telling children that there are no monsters may not ease the fear of a child who "knows" that there is one under his bed. When information and explanations are not appropriate, an idea for helping to reduce a child's fears is to engage the child in imaginative, fun ways of facing the fear. Some examples follow.

> *For a fear of monsters under the bed, provide a spray bottle of Monster Spray (water).*

> *For a fear of thunder, have children help you make up a story about the source of the noise, for example, giants bowling in the clouds.*

■ Help children stand up for what they believe in and praise them when they do so. For example, if children see or hear others taunting and teasing a classmate, encourage them to refrain from "joining the crowd" or even to step up and speak against it. Peer pressure is a hard thing to stand against. Praise children when they stand firm.

Activities for older children

■ Model holding to your convictions. For example, if you are an animal-rights advocate and you learn that a company whose products you've been using relies on animal testing, stop using their products—even if changing to a new line is uncomfortable or less convenient. Write or phone the "old" company and let them know that you will no longer support them. Explain to your children, as simply as possible, what you are doing and why. The courage of our convictions is not always as easy to hold as we might hope.

■ Help children stand up for what they believe in. For example, if children are concerned about the environment, encourage them to approach the principal with a school-wide recycling plan. It takes a lot of courage to stand up to authority and to implement change. Tell children how proud you are that they can hold to their convictions.

The Values Book

Books to Share With Children

Read books that illustrate and advocate courage. Check your library for some of those listed here. Each one provides opportunities to discuss facing fears.

All by Myself by Anna Grossnickle Hines
Anna Banana and Me by Lenore Blegvad
The Buffalo Jump by Peter Roop
The Gates of the Wind by Kathryn Lasky
Harriet and the Roller Coaster by Nancy Carlson
Harry and the Terrible Whatzit by Dick Gackenbach
A House by the River by William Miller
Ira Sleeps Over by Bernard Waber
Keep the Lights Burning, Abbie by Peter Roop and Connie Roop
Little Rabbit's Loose Tooth by Lucy Bate
Oliver Button Is a Sissy by Tomie dePaola
The Something by Natalie Babbit
Tacky the Penguin by Helen Lester
There's a Nightmare in My Closet by Mercer Mayer
Thundercake by Patricia Polacco
White Socks Only by Evelyn Coleman

Determination &
Commitment

The itsy bitsy spider went up the waterspout.
Down came the rain and washed the spider out.
Out came the sun and dried up all the rain.
And the itsy bitsy spider went up the spout again.

Determination & Commitment

What Are Determination and Commitment?

Commitment binds us to our

ideals, to our work and to each

other. It is our pledge to hold fast

to our own beliefs and

pursuits and to support and stick

by our family and friends.

Determination enables us to

achieve our goals.

Why Are Determination and Commitment Important? Things for Adults to Think About

■ Determination and commitment create the bond in friendships. They allow us to hang on to a friend despite difficulties, disagreements and disillusionment.

Think about your friends. How would you feel if you disagreed? Would you work it out? Why?

■ Determination and commitment make it possible for us to realize our goals. There would be no telephone, no hope for children with polio, no early childhood classrooms without the commitment and dedication of those individuals who were able to stay with their goals despite the boredom, difficulties and setbacks that their commitments required.

Where would we be as a society with no Alexander Graham Bells, Maria Montessoris or Jonas Salks in our future?

■ We have become a "throw away" society. If a toy breaks, we throw it away. If the job gets difficult, we quit. We exchange toys and jobs (and sometimes relationships) for new ones, and then we repeat the cycle.

Brainstorm a list of by-products of being a "throw away" society. How do you feel about each one?

■ Determination and commitment keep us focused. If we are determined to be honest, for example, we are far less likely to change our behavior or direction when an opportunity to be dishonest presents itself.

How do you feel about stealing? Are there times when it would be okay to steal?

Talking With Children About Determination and Commitment

Are determination and commitment values worth keeping? Talk with children about the questions below and see what they think.

■ Think about a time when you worked on something that took a long time. How did you feel when you were finished? Happy? Proud?

■ What does it mean to be a friend? Is a friend someone you can count on?

■ With young children, sing "The Itsy Bitsy Spider" and do the hand motions. Talk about how the spider just wouldn't give up; she was washed down by the rain but crawled right back up again. The spider was committed to her plan of getting up that spout.

■ Do you belong to a group like a dance class or swimming class? Has there ever been a time when you didn't want to go to class? What happened? What happens when you go to class and someone else isn't there? How do you feel about that?

■ Think about a game you like to play with your friends. Has anyone ever stopped playing before the game was finished? How did you feel about that?

Develop children's language skills and continue the discussion of determination and commitment by weaving the following vocabulary words into your day.

bond	determination
caring	disappointment
commitment	goals
completion	progress
decision	setbacks

Things to Do in the Classroom

Activities for children of all ages

■ Sing songs that support the concept of sticking with our goals, like "High Hopes" and "Inch by Inch."

++*+*+* The Values Book

■ Encourage children to finish the projects they begin. For example, they should work a puzzle at least once before they put it away, build one structure with the blocks before they abandon them, play one round of a game before allowing a player to quit.

Children need to learn that projects require thinking through from the beginning and that once a decision is made to begin a project, completing it is part of the process. In our effort to provide children with choices, we have somehow lost sight of the fact that choices have results and consequences. If children are allowed to choose quitting a project before completion, they never experience the pride and satisfaction that come with finishing what they begin.

■ Plan projects that require several steps to complete. Be sure that children finish their part of each project.

Grow plants in the classroom. Let the children select the plants they want, plant the seeds, care for the plants and monitor their growth.

Let children raise a class pet like a baby rabbit. Make sure children share the responsibilities of taking care of the animal just as they will share in the enjoyment of having it in the classroom.

Determination & Commitment

Do a cooking project. You may want to prepare a pot of soup or make bread from scratch.

Vegetable Soup

3 medium tomatoes
3 carrots
3 stalks of celery with tops
1 medium onion
3 medium potatoes

10 oz. (300 g) package frozen peas
3 cups (750 ml) water
1 teaspoon (5 ml) salt
1 teaspoon (5 ml) pepper
3 beef bouillon cubes

cutting board
peeler
sharp knife and table knife
measuring cup and spoons
large spoon
crock pot
bowls and spoons

1. Wash, peel and cut the tomatoes. Put into the crock pot.
2. Wash, peel, slice and add the carrots.
3. Wash, slice and add the celery.
4. Wash, peel, cut and add the onion.
5. Wash, peel, cut and add the potatoes.
6. Open box and add the frozen peas.
7. Add the 3 cups of water.
8. Add the salt and pepper.
9. Add the 3 beef bouillon cubes.
10. Stir the soup.
11. Plug in the crock pot and cook on HIGH for 4-6 hours. When the soup is ready, pour into bowls or cups and enjoy!

Reprinted from THE GIANT ENCYCLOPEDIA OF THEME ACTIVITIES FOR CHILDREN 2 TO 5 (Gryphon House, 1993)

The Values Book

Yummy Yeast Bread

1-2 tablespoons (15-30 ml) active dry yeast
1/3 cup plus 1 teaspoon (75 ml + 5 ml) honey
warm water
1 teaspoon (5 ml) salt
1/3 cup (75 ml) oil, plus a little extra for greasing the bowl and pan(s)
6 cups (1.2 kg) whole wheat flour, supplemented as needed

small mixing bowl
two large bowls
wooden spoons
measuring spoons and cups
wooden board or clean table top
clean cloth
two loaf pans or baking trays
oven

1. In a small bowl, mix the yeast, 1 teaspoon honey and 1/2 cup warm water. Allow this mixture to sit until it gets bubbly—approximately ten minutes.
2. In a large bowl, mix 1 1/2 cups (375 ml) warm water, 1/3 cup oil, 1/3 cup honey and salt.
3. Pour the yeast mixture into the large bowl and stir in three cups of whole wheat flour. Mix well, and continue adding more flour until the dough is fairly stiff and not sticky (possibly as much as three more cups of flour).
4. Turn the dough onto a lightly floured board or clean table top and begin to knead, firmly pressing the dough away from you with the heels of your hands, folding it back onto itself and pressing it away from you again. Continue rhythmically kneading the dough until it becomes smooth and elastic.
5. Place in an oiled bowl, cover with a clean cloth and let rise on a sunny window sill or in another warm place until it doubles in bulk (about 45 minutes).
6. Punch down (press down two or three times firmly but gently with your fists). Shape into two loaves or 24 small rolls (approximately). Cover and let rise once more for about 20-30 minutes.
7. Bake at 350°F (180°C) for 45-50 minutes for bread or 20 minutes for rolls.
Note: You can leave out one or both risings (steps five and six) if you want to eat the bread or rolls for snack the same day. Just roll handfuls of dough into balls and place them on an oiled cookie sheet. Bake right away for warm, fresh rolls in 20 minutes. Make sure to let cool a bit before eating.

Reprinted from EARTHWAYS by Carol Petrash
(Gryphon House, 1992)

Determination & Commitment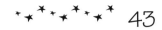

■ Add an unfinished project box to the art center. Encourage children to put their projects in a folder in the box and go back to them the next day.

■ Share one of your projects like knitting, needlepoint, painting, sewing or woodworking as a model for children. Discuss how you developed the project from beginning to end. Be sure to tell about any setbacks or disappointments you encountered. You may even want to show your project at different stages. That way children can see the progression and completion.

Working With Families: Ideas for Home

Activities for children of all ages

■ When toys break, try to fix them. If they can't be fixed, try to use their parts for something else. Do not just toss and replace.

■ Demonstrate determination and commitment in all you do. Stick to your own projects, stay focused on your goals and endure setbacks with determination. Our actions speak louder than our words.

■ Let children solve their own problems. You can listen and offer advice when asked, but children need to practice brainstorming alternatives, selecting an option, trying it out and evaluating its success. Many times failure to keep a commitment is really giving up in the face of a problem.

Ask children open-ended questions to help them through the process.

Can you tell me about the problem?
What ways can you think of to solve the problem?
What will you need to solve the problem?
What will you do if your solution doesn't work?
How will you know if the problem is solved?

■ When disagreements occur between family members, encourage them to negotiate a peaceful resolution, instead of intervening yourself. For example, if siblings are arguing about which television program to watch, have them identify a solution. They might alternate viewing times, one choosing today and the other tomorrow. They might make a trade for something they want to watch later. They might record one channel and view the other. Willingness to work things out shows commitment to each other.

The Values Book

■ Set aside some time the family can commit to and create a special family time or ritual. This can be dinner together on a specific day each week, Friday night videos and popcorn or Sunday afternoon board games.

Activities for older children

■ When children sign up for an activity like dancing lessons, or swimming lessons, be sure they stay involved until a reasonable or logical quitting point. For example, if they join a club and then decide they don't like it, insist they stay for at least a semester. Sometimes staying for a while changes their initial reaction. Check your local listings for organizations such as the YMCA or YWCA that may offer activities for your child.

■ When children begin a project, whether it's building a fort or writing a letter to grandparents, make sure they finish it.

■ When children fail at a project, help them evaluate what went wrong.

Did they bite off more than they could chew?
Was the project too big to begin with?
Did they start off without a plan?
Did they fail to check their resources?

Help children find a lesson they can learn from the experience and encourage them to try again.

Books to Share With Children

Read books that illustrate and encourage determination and commitment. Check your library for some of those listed here. Each one provides opportunities to discuss the results of staying with our efforts.

Amazing Grace by Mary Hoffman
Angus and the Cat by Marjorie Flack
Aunt Chip and the Great Triple Creek Dam Affair by Patricia Polacco
Believing Sophie by Hazel Hatchins
Brave Irene by William Steig
The Carrot Seed by Ruth Kraus
Horton Hatches the Egg by Dr. Seuss
Inch by Inch by David Mallett
The Itsy Bitsy Spider by Iza Trapani
The Little Engine That Could by Watty Piper
The Little Red Hen by Paul Galdone
Mike Mulligan and His Steam Shovel by Virginia Lee Burton

Fairness

Trot, trot to Boston town
To get a stick of candy.
One for you, one for me,
And one for Dicky Dandy.

Fairness

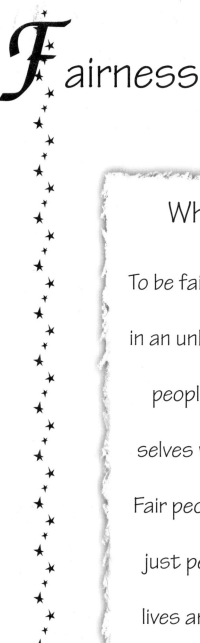

What Is Fairness?

To be fair we must regard others in an unbiased manner and treat people equitably, as we ourselves would like to be treated. Fair people maintain an honest, just perspective in their daily lives and in special situations.

Why Is Fairness Important? Things for Adults to Think About

■ The Golden Rule—do unto others as you would have them do unto you—is founded on the principle of fairness.

Was the Golden Rule important to you as a child? Is it now? When was the last time you applied this rule with conscious thought?

■ Circumstances can create unfairness. Let's say you interview for a job, and another applicant—less qualified, but a friend of the boss—gets the job. Would you feel you had been treated fairly?

List situations and circumstances in your life that have resulted in unfairness. Think of a time when you made a decision or acted in a way that wasn't based on applying rules equitably.

■ Fairness can be a controversial, even volatile subject. With people from many cultures and backgrounds trying to live together and share resources, it's not uncommon to have groups feel that they are being discriminated against. That cry of discrimination comes from a feeling of being treated unfairly.

Think of recent situations where a group claimed discrimination. Can you trace their feelings to issues of fairness?

■ Children's understanding of fairness is very different from adults' understanding. Children see things in black and white while most adults see variations of black and white (gray).

For example, the class rule is that children may sit wherever they wish during circle time. However, you always ask Garrett to sit next to you during story circle because experience tells you that if he's not next to you he'll be disruptive. Garrett sees the situation as unfair because he has an assigned seat while the other children get to choose their seats. On the other hand, the other children might see the situation as unfair because Garrett always gets to sit next to the teacher.

You have a good reason for altering the rule, but unless you state that reason to the children, they see your action as arbitrary and unfair. When we make exceptions to rules, we must explain our reasoning to children so they begin to broaden their understanding of fairness.

How would you handle this situation so that Garrett and the other children see the seating arrangement as fair? Would you allow Garrett to be disruptive before bringing him to sit next to you each time?

■ When children act defiantly, it's usually because they perceive something to be unfair. For example, a child in the classroom who is constantly being reprimanded, even before a situation has been assessed to identify the guilty parties, begins to feel picked on. A child who has a brand new baby brother or sister often feels left out and pushed aside. These children may act out in frustration.

Have you ever been treated unfairly? How did you feel? How did you react?

■ Should rules be based on individual situations and circumstances or should they always be the same for everyone? What about the difference in bedtimes for an older and a younger child? Should rules be the same for females and males?

If you grew up with siblings, how were the rules in your family established? Did you think they were fair then? Has your opinion changed as an adult?

■ One of the best ways for a child to learn fairness is through observing and practicing good sportsmanship. One of the first things we learn in athletics is that playing fairly and being a good sport are more important than winning. Recently there have been examples of this philosophy being replaced with an attitude of winning at all costs. Just before the 1996 World Series, a player was reprimanded for spitting in the umpire's face. The rules called for an immediate suspension. However, because the player was on a team headed for the playoffs, the Baseball Commission postponed his suspension until the World Series was over.

Do you think people should turn their heads the other way if following the rules means losing the game? What conclusions do you think children draw from this kind of behavior?

■ People make judgments and decisions based on their biases and prejudices. The guilt or innocence of a suspected criminal is often decided before the trial begins. Many of us form opinions about the mental, moral and physical abilities of others based solely on their race, gender, ethnicity or lifestyle.

Have you ever been in a situation where you felt that others judged you without knowing you? If the result were negative would you think it was unfair? What if it were positive? Would you still think it was unfair?

Talking With Children About Fairness

Is fairness a value worth keeping? Talk with children about the questions below and see what they think.

■ What does fair mean?

■ Do you feel like you're treated fairly at home? At school? How do you feel when someone treats you unfairly?

■ With young children, say the "Trot, trot to Boston town" poem. Talk about how much fun it can be to share with our friends and to treat each other fairly, or equitably.

■ Is it okay to cheat to win a game? Why or why not? Would it be okay for someone else to cheat to beat you in a game?

■ Do you think it's fair that older children get to stay up later and do more things than younger children? Why or why not?

Develop children's language skills and continue the discussion of fairness by weaving the following vocabulary words into your day.

fairness	just
honesty	justice
cheating	injustice
dishonest	rules
equitable	unfair

Things to Do in the Classroom

Activities for children of all ages

■ Provide opportunities for children to practice taking turns.

Use a helper chart for assigned duties.
Use an egg timer for sharing materials and equipment.
Play games that require taking turns.

■ Read *The Doorbell Rang* by Pat Hutchins. Brainstorm ways to divide the cookies fairly each time the doorbell rings. Children might enjoy acting out this story.

■ Play games with simple rules, such as Tic-Tac-Toe; Duck, Duck, Goose; and Hide-and-Seek.

■ Let children make up the classroom rules. Help them keep the list short and simple. After they have made their suggestions, see if those suggestions could be contained in one general rule, such as, "Don't do anything to hurt yourself or anyone else." Ask children to test their individual suggestions against the one rule. Does it work? Is it fair? Whether you have one rule or many, make sure they are followed and enforced fairly and consistently.

■ Watch for children who act defiantly. If you have defiant children, try to get them to express their feelings. If they say that they are being treated unfairly, examine their complaints carefully. If you look at the situation from their perspective, you may understand their feelings. If children are being treated unfairly, take corrective measures.

■ Rules need to be consistent. If you find it necessary to alter a rule, be sure to explain your decision to the children.

⋆⋆*⋆*⋆*   The Values Book

Activities for older children

■ Bring in a cake and ask the children to figure out how to divide it fairly. Then try it. Cut the cake into pieces large enough for two children. Pair the children. Give each pair one piece of cake and one plastic knife. Direct each pair to let one child cut the cake and the other be the first to choose a piece. Are they careful to be fair? To cut equal pieces?

■ Encourage children to play board games like checkers, Parcheesi and Monopoly. Remind them that playing fairly means following the rules at all times. What would happen if there were no rules?

■ Encourage children to play a game with no rules. Is it possible? Ask them to make up new rules for a familiar game and play it that way. Are the rules fair? Finally, try this. Play the game again with one player or team following the traditional set of rules and another using the new rules. What happens?

Working With Families: Ideas for Home

Activities for children of all ages

■ Model fairness in activities around the house. For example, share the television, share responsibilities of cooking and cleaning up, share your time.

■ Refrain from making statements such as, "Because I said so," "Because I'm the adult" and "Because that's just the way it is." Children deserve explanations for why things are the way they are, and you need to remember that just because you're big, you're not always right. Fairness has nothing to do with size, age or position.

■ Use helper charts to determine whose responsibility it is to wash the car, mow the lawn, wash the dishes, vacuum and dust.

■ Help children establish positive self-esteem. Children who feel good about themselves pro-actively seek solutions to challenges. Children who don't feel good about themselves blame their situation on someone or something else. They feel that the world treats them unfairly.

Help children develop a positive outlook. You can't manipulate others' sense of fairness, but you can help them keep a balance by encouraging them to focus on the many fair things in life as opposed to the few unfair things.

■ Pose problems and encourage children to find fair solutions to them. For example, two children spot a tricycle and run over to it at the same time. What would be a fair way to decide who rides it first? Three children have one sandwich between them. How can each child get a fair share? Sometimes these scenarios provide great themes for puppet shows.

The Values Book

Activities for older children

■ If you have more than one child, be careful not to make the older child a primary caretaker or baby-sitter of the younger one.

■ If your children are involved in sports, make sure your words and your actions convey the message that playing fairly is more important than winning.

■ When your child says that you are being unfair or that a sibling is being unfair, try a role reversal to examine and settle the situation.

■ Model working for fairness and justice. Join a cause that fights injustice. For example, you could contact the Southern Poverty Law Center at (334) 264-0286, Amnesty International at (212) 633-4200 or Save the Children at (203) 221-4000.

Books to Share With Children

Read books that illustrate and encourage fairness. Check your library for some of those listed here. Each one provides opportunities to discuss the results of fair and equitable behavior.

Boggin, Blizzy, and Sleeter the Cheater by Michael P. Waite
Dance, Tanya by Patricia Gauch
The Day Gogo Went to Vote by Elinor Batezat Sisulu
The Doorbell Rang by Pat Hutchins
Finding the Greenstone by Alice Walker
Jamaica's Blue Marker by Juanita Havill
"The Lion and the Mouse" by Aesop (many versions available)
"The Little Red Hen."(many versions available)
Old Henry by Joan Blos
Roxaboxen by Alice McLerran
What Will Mommy Do When I'm At School? by Delores Johnson
You're the Boss, Baby Duck! by Amy Hest

Helpfulness

I had a little dog
His name was Fido.
He was nothing but a pup.
He could stand up on his hind legs
If I held his front legs up.

Helpfulness

What Is Helpfulness?

Helpfulness is the practice of

aiding and assisting others. It

is also an attitude we can

cultivate by always being ready

to lend a hand, by actively

looking for opportunities to make

a contribution.

Why Is Helpfulness Important? Things for Adults to Think About

■ Being helpful to one another was a way of life in early America. As industry and technology made us more self-sufficient, the need for help from our neighbors diminished.

Think of ways you could be helpful to your friends and neighbors. How do you think your friends and neighbors would react to your helpfulness?

■ Time magazine publishes a weekly column of stories about ordinary people who find ways to make a difference by helping others.

Can you think of examples of everyday heroes?

■ Many people have jobs that center around helping others, such as firefighters, doctors, teachers and garbage collectors.

What other occupations can you think of that provide help to others? Are there any parts of your job that provide service or assistance to other people?

■ Sometimes people are hesitant to help others because they're afraid to get involved or afraid of being injured.

Look through a newspaper to find stories about people who witnessed a crime but didn't get involved. Then look for stories about people who helped others.

■ When is the last time you worked in a homeless shelter or participated in a fund-raiser?

If you haven't done any charitable work recently, ask yourself why.

Talking With Children About Helpfulness

Is helpfulness a value worth keeping? Talk with children about the questions below and see what they think.

■ Can you think of things you could do that would be helpful to your family or friends? Can you think of things they could do that would be helpful to you?

■ Brainstorm reasons for helping each other. If children respond, "So he'll like me" and "So I'll get a reward," help them look beyond their own needs. Help children understand the sense of community established by helping.

■ With young children, say the poem about Fido (children could act this out). Talk about how, in helping the pup to stand on his hind legs, the child has had fun, too.

■ Who are some characters in books who help others? What are some of the things they do that are helpful?

Develop children's language skills and continue the discussion of helpfulness by weaving the following vocabulary words into your day.

appreciate	help
assist	helpful
charity	kindness
community	opportunity
giving	useful

Things to Do in the Classroom

Activities for children of all ages

■ Establish and maintain a helpful attitude in the classroom. Keep the motto "One for all and all for one."

■ Encourage children to help each other instead of automatically running to you for help. For example, children can help each other put on their painting smocks, tie each other's shoes, help hang artwork and brainstorm solutions to problems.

■ Do group projects such as building a tower, creating a mural or cooking a pot of soup (see page 42 for a soup recipe). Talk about the role each person plays in helping to complete the project.

■ Tell add-on stories. One person starts the story, the next picks it up and adds on. Talk about how the story that everyone helps to create is different from a story that one person makes up.

■ Raise money for a charity or organize a clothing or food drive. See the chapter on Cooperation for more suggestions. Be sure children are with you when you make the donation.

■ Invite children to make a list of things they still need help doing. Is the list shorter or longer than when they were babies? Make a list of things children can do to help each other.

Need Help	Help each other
• cutting	• Tying shoes
• cooking food	• putting on paint smocks
• making bed	• picking up toys
• building a tower	• building a tower
• picking up toys	• making a picture

Helpfulness

Activities for older children

■ Visit a retirement home. Prearrange things the children can do that could be helpful, like planting a garden or hanging artwork in each room.

■ Note the days or weeks that are designated for increasing national awareness and appreciation for community helpers. Encourage the children to brainstorm ways they can show their appreciation, such as baking cookies for or sending letters of support to the designated group. *Celebrate Today!* by John Kremer lists special days of recognition in a monthly format. You can order a copy from Prima Publishing, P. O. Box 1260 BK, Rocklin, CA 95677. Or, check your local library for a copy of *Chase's Annual Events,* which lists all holidays and special days of recognition and explains the origins of each holiday.

■ Look for and take advantage of opportunities for older children to help younger children. For example, older children could tutor or read to younger children or teach them how to play a new game. Sometimes older children finish their work early; helping children in a younger class is a good fill-in activity. Both groups learn something about helpfulness.

Working With Families: Ideas for Home

Activities for children of all ages

■ Model helpfulness in your daily routine. Open doors for each other, offer to carry something, volunteer to bring a drink to someone on your way from the kitchen. Be sure to express your appreciation for each other.

■ Help each other with chores. Dividing the work gets the job done faster, and having company usually makes it fun.

■ Help your neighbors. Have house painting parties or lawn care parties. Be sure to involve your children. Everyone needs a job to do.

■ Volunteer at your child's school.

Activities for older children

■ Join a service organization like the Camp Fire Boys and Girls. Check your local listings for phone numbers, or call the Camp Fire Boys and Girls by calling their national headquarters at (800) 669-6884. Organizations like these provide ample opportunities for being helpful to others.

■ Have the whole family volunteer to work in a homeless shelter. You may have an opportunity to make beds, serve meals or play with the children. Be certain your children can play a substantial role.

■ Participate in a service project together, such as a community park cleanup, a Habitat for Humanity project (call 1-800-HUMANITY for more information), or a Sierra Club service trip (call Sierra Club National Headquarters at (415) 977-5500).

Books to Share With Children

Read books that illustrate and encourage helpfulness. Check your library for some of those listed here. Each one provides opportunities to discuss the results of giving aid and assistance.

Amos and Boris by William Steig
Can I Help? by Marilyn Janowitz
"The Great Big Turnip" (many versions available)
Helping Out by George Ancona
Henrietta's First Winter by Rob Lewis
Herman the Helper by Robert Kraus
I Like to Help by Karen Erickson and Maureen Roffey
Island Baby by Holly Keller
Is Susan Here? by Janice Udry
The Legend of the Poinsettia by Tomie dePaola
"The Lion and the Mouse" by Aesop (many versions available)
"The Little Red Hen" (many versions available)
Manners by Aliki
Mommies Don't Get Sick by Marilyn Hafner
"The Shoemaker and the Elves" (many versions available)
Wilfrid Gordon McDonald Partridge by Mem Fox

Honesty &
Integrity

Whene'er you make a promise,
Consider well its importance.
And when made,
Engrave it upon your heart.

Honesty & Integrity

What Are Honesty and Integrity?

We practice honesty when we

speak truthfully and treat

others fairly. We possess

integrity when we are honest

with ourselves, holding to our

own code of moral values.

Why Are Honesty and Integrity Important? Things for Adults to Think About

■ There was a time when Americans prided themselves on their honesty and integrity. We believed our government and our neighbor to be honest. Our word was our bond.

When was the first time you doubted the truth of the above statement?

■ Our society has traditionally counted on public figures (politicians, athletes, actors) to be role models. Since the actions of so many of today's role models reveal a lack of honesty and integrity, where might we find new role models?

When you were a child, who were your role models for honesty and integrity? Do they have counterparts in today's society?

■ Honesty is the basis of trust. Trust is the basis of relationships, whether they be personal or business.

Do you know someone who has a good relationship that lacks trust?

■ Young children have trouble distinguishing between fact and fantasy. They may misrepresent facts because they haven't yet developed the ability to distinguish facts. They may even believe that changing the facts in their heads changes the facts in reality. Honesty is a developing concept for children younger than seven. They need experience with honesty in order to learn how to employ it.

Think of a time you tried to get a straight answer from a young child. Did you end up confused? Think how confused they might be with the stories of Santa Claus, the Tooth Fairy and the Easter Bunny.

■ Many of us grew up with the motto, "Honesty is the best policy."

Can you think of a time when honesty might not be the best policy? If you changed your motto, would relationships be harmed? Would you feel okay about yourself? How would you feel if the tables were turned and someone close to you no longer valued honesty?

Talking With Children About Honesty and Integrity

Are honesty and integrity values worth keeping? Talk with children about the ideas below and see what they think.

■ What is honesty? What is the difference between the truth and a lie? Tell me the difference.

■ Has anyone ever told you something that wasn't true? If so, how did it make you feel? Do you trust that person to tell you the truth now? Why or why not?

■ Read this chapter's opening poem to the children. Talk about promises the children have made or promises others have made to them. How serious is a promise? How does it feel when someone breaks a promise to you?

■ Have you ever worried about telling the truth about something because you thought it would get you into trouble?

■ Who are the most honest people you know? How do you know they are honest? How do you feel about these people?

Develop children's language skills and continue the discussion of honesty and integrity by weaving the following vocabulary words into your day.

fact	trust
fantasy	trustworthy
honesty	truth
integrity	untrue
promise	untrustworthy

Things to Do in the Classroom

Activities for children of all ages

■ Use literature to help children distinguish between fact and fantasy. Because they lack experiential background, young children have difficulty determining what is real and unreal. For example, young children don't know if a wolf can blow down a house because they have no experience with wolves. Around the age of seven, children usually have acquired enough information to begin to separate fact from fantasy.

Play Fact or Fantasy. Give children a red paper circle and a green paper circle. The green circle signals go and the red circle signals stop. Start telling a made-up story. Have the children hold up the green circle until you say something that couldn't really happen. Then they hold up the red circle to stop you. Continue the story using the signals for facts and fantasies.

Discuss real and make-believe situations in books that you read in the classroom. Encourage the children to tell how they know something is real or make-believe.

Encourage children to tell a story that is completely fantasy. Then have them tell a story that is completely factual.

■ When children distort the truth, help them sort through the facts. Explain to them how important it is to get the facts straight so that people will be able to trust what they say.

■ Support children when their beliefs are different from your own. Don't force them to think like you in order to receive your approval. If their thinking is unsound, help guide them to more rational thought without belittling them. If children are going to be able to stand up for what they believe in, they will need support from both teachers and parents.

Activities for older children

■ When children are playing board games, talk about the importance of playing fairly and honestly. What happens to a game if someone cheats? If you cheat to win, can you really count it as winning?

■ Help children see the long-term effects of dishonesty by presenting them with situations that illustrate the burden of misrepresenting the truth. For example, if you stand on your tiptoes when you're measured this year, will you have to stand on your tiptoes from now on?

Working With Families: Ideas for Home

Activities for children of all ages

■ Support children saying what they believe even when it is different from what you believe. You may want to attempt to redirect their thinking, but don't expect them to say something because it is what they know you want to hear. This is tough, but it lays the ground work for honesty.

■ In the same regard, don't expect children to do something they don't feel like doing just to save face. For example, don't make Alyssa say she is sorry if she isn't, and don't make Austin kiss his Aunt Rose if he doesn't want to. Making children

The Values Book

perform acts that are void of meaning only causes them to develop dishonest actions. Model the behavior you want them to imitate.

■ Model honesty. Don't tell the neighbors how much you like what they did with their flower bed, then go inside and tell your spouse how bad it looks. If a clerk gives you too much change, return the difference. If the cable company doesn't know you're getting service, tell them and start paying for it.

■ When you catch children being dishonest about a matter that isn't trivial, help them understand the long-term consequences. For example, when you tell a lie, you have to remember every detail of the lie and who you told it to, possibly for the rest of your life. What a burden!

Activities for older children

■ When children are dishonest, help them sort through the facts of what happened without anger or judgments. Sometimes they just need to take a closer look.

■ When the opportunity arises, talk with children about intangible things that can be stolen. For example, is it stealing to take credit for someone else's work?

■ Watch a movie, such as *The Lion King*, *Pinocchio* or *Monkey Trouble*, in which honesty and truthfulness are major themes. Encourage your child to talk about ways the main characters demonstrate honesty (and dishonesty).

Books to Share With Children

Read books that illustrate and encourage honesty and integrity. Check your library for some of those listed here. Each one provides opportunities to discuss honesty and integrity.

A Day's Work by Eve Bunting
Believing Sophie by Hazel Hutchins
The Empty Pot by Demi
Ernie's Little Lie by Dan Elliott
Fernando's Gift by Douglas Keister
Harriet and the Garden by Nancy Carlson
Liar, Liar, Pants on Fire! by Miriam Cohen
Loudmouth George and the Fishing Trip by Nancy Carlson
Read for Me, Mama by Vashanti Rahaman
The True Story of the Three Little Pigs by Jon Scieszka
We're Going on a Bear Hunt by Michael Rosen

Humor

Down by the bay
Where the watermelons grow
Back to my home
I dare not go.
For if I do,
My mother will say,
"Did you ever see a bear combing his hair
down by the bay?"

Humor

What Is Humor?

Humor can brighten our daily

lives as we smile at amusing

occurrences, laugh at silly

situations and chuckle at

absurdities. It is our ability to

perceive and appreciate comedy

in our world and in ourselves.

Why Is Humor Important? Things for Adults to Think About

■ As the world has gotten more complex and serious, our humor has become more sophisticated and, therefore, more difficult for children to understand. Catching on to humor requires a wide range of experience and understanding. You can't know what's out of whack if you don't have a point of reference.

Watch cartoons with children. Mark the number of statements and actions ("gags") that go over their heads.

■ Humor takes time to nurture and develop. We're not born with it; we have to acquire it.

What's the earliest joke you can recall? Is it funny to you today? Do your children think it's funny?

■ The more egocentric we are in our thinking, the less likely we are to see humor in certain situations. Humor requires that we look beyond ourselves and that we be able to laugh at ourselves.

When was the last time you had a good laugh at yourself?

■ What is humorous to one person may be offensive to someone else. For example, racial and political jokes are told at someone's expense.

Can humor go too far?

■ Humor can get us through the tough times and the rough times.

Think of a situation when you relied on humor to get you through.

Talking With Children About Humor

Is humor a value worth keeping? Talk with children about the ideas below and see what they think.

■ Tell me the funniest joke you know. What makes it so funny?

■ What makes clowns funny?

■ Sing or recite "Down by the Bay" with young children. Sing the song again, each time ending with one of the following lines:

"Did you ever see a goose kissing a moose down by the bay?"
"Did you ever see a bee with a sunburned knee down by the bay?"
"Did you ever see a whale with a polka-dot tail down by the bay?"

Talk about the verses that make us laugh—are they things that could really happen (a goose kissing a moose, etc.) or are they nonsense?

■ What is something funny that you do? What funny things do your friends do?

■ Who is the funniest person you know? What does that person do that is funny?

■ Which book or cartoon or show on TV do you think is the funniest? Why is it so funny?

Develop children's language skills and continue the discussion of humor by weaving the following vocabulary words into your day.

exaggeration	laughter
funny	nonsense
humor	riddle
humorous	serious
joke	silly

Things to Do in the Classroom

Activities for children of all ages

■ Teach children other humorous songs, such as "One Elephant" and "Annie Mae." A good collection of humorous songs is *Wee Sing Silly Songs* by Pamela Conn Beall and Susan Hagen Nipp (Price Stern Sloan, 1986).

The Values Book

■ Read books that encourage more than one way of looking at something, such as *The King Who Rained* and *A Chocolate Moose for Dinner*.

■ Have a Wacky Wednesday or Backwards Day. Encourage wacky thinking and outrageous exaggerations. You may want to use the book *Wacky Wednesday* by Theodore LeSieg to launch your fun.

■ Let children see you laugh at yourself. When you get your words mixed up or get mixed up on the daily schedule, laugh at yourself.

■ Pay attention to children's literal interpretations of vocabulary and help them learn the multiple meanings of words. For example, ask children for their interpretations of "the fork in the road," "I have a frog in my throat," "you drive me up the wall" and other common expressions. It would be fun to have the children illustrate their interpretations.

Humor

■ Encourage diverse answers. There's more than one way to see most things. The more legitimate answers children can come up with, the easier it will be for them to recognize answers that are slightly off the wall.

■ Play nonsense games. Ask questions such as, "What would happen if an octopus had wings instead of arms?" "What would happen if you put an elephant and a giraffe together? What would you call it? What would be funny about it?"

Activities for older children

■ Encourage older children to visit younger children and share jokes. Their jokes sound relatively unsophisticated to adults, but they can help raise the level of comprehension in the younger children.

■ Read a Dr. Seuss book, such as *Green Eggs and Ham* or *The Cat in the Hat.* Invite children to create story extensions using the same language patterns and humor.

Working With Families: Ideas for Home

Activities for children of all ages

■ Laugh at yourself when you do or say something that embarrasses you. Encourage your children to laugh at themselves.

■ Laugh at your children's attempts at being funny. If they put on a skit or say, "Hey, look at me!" to solicit your laughter, accommodate them.

■ Do things backwards. Eat dinner from dessert to salad or walk backwards to the mailbox.

■ Break routines. Be spontaneous. For example, if an ice-cream sundae sounds good for breakfast, have one. Invite others to join you. If you've watched videos and ordered pizza the past six Friday nights, try something different like miniature golf and a peanut butter and jelly sandwich picnic.

■ Watch television with your child. Discuss the humor when it occurs.

■ Read the funny papers to your child.

The Values Book

■ Sit in front of a mirror together and make funny faces. Who can bug their eyes out the farthest? Who can open their mouth the widest? Who can make the funniest face?

■ Reserve a space on your refrigerator door for displaying funny pictures and snapshots.

■ Share things that made you laugh during the day. Try to remember at least one thing each day; work your way up to more.

Activities for older children

■ Make up riddles, limericks and simple puns with your children.

■ Share jokes with your children.

Books to Share With Children

Read books that illustrate and encourage a sense of humor. Check your library for some of those listed here. Each one provides opportunities to discuss the results of looking on the lighter side.

The Cat in the Hat by Dr. Seuss
A Chocolate Moose for Dinner by Fred Gwynne
Fish Out of Water by Helen Palmer
The Frances Books by Russell Hoban
Green Eggs and Ham by Dr. Seuss
The King Who Rained by Fred Gwynne
The Monster at the End of This Book by Sesame Street Staff
Muddle Cuddle by Laurel Dee Gugler
My Dog Never Says Please by Suzanne Williams
The Pig in the Pond by Martin Waddell
Silly Sally by Audrey Wood
The Stupid Books by Harry Allard
Wacky Wednesday by Theodore Le Sieg
Wee Sing Silly Songs by Pamela Conn Beall and Susan Hagen Nipp
Why a Disguise? by Laura Numeroff

The Values Book

Independence &
Self-Reliance

This is the way I brush my teeth,
Brush my teeth, brush my teeth.
This is the way I brush my teeth,
So early in the morning.

Independence & Self-Reliance

What Are Independence and Self-Reliance?

The freedom to exercise our own personal competence is independence. Through self-reliance we can negotiate our own path in this world—weighing our choices and making our own decisions.

Why Are Independence and Self-Reliance Important? Things for Adults to Think About

■ Children are born totally dependent on adults to provide for their needs, but their ultimate survival depends on their learning to be self-sufficient and independent.

Think of ways we encourage children to walk, talk, feed themselves and so on. Do you know people who prefer to keep their children dependent? Why do some people hang on to dependency and what effect does it have on the child?

■ A healthy individual is independent yet respects the interdependence humankind needs for survival.

Think of things you depend on other people for. Could you do any of these things independently?

■ Think about the number of children who are drawn to gangs. If you listen to what children say about their gang orientation, the impetus seems to be their wanting to belong to a family. When family connections are strong, it creates a base, a safety net allowing children to experiment with and develop independent behavior.

Look for examples in your neighborhood of children who have strong family connections and those who don't. Which children display stronger, healthier, independent behaviors?

Talking With Children About Independence and Self-Reliance

Are independence and self-reliance values worth keeping? Talk with children about the following ideas and see what they think.

■ Name some things you can do all by yourself. How does being able to do these things make you feel?

■ Name some things that you want to be able to do all by yourself. How will you learn to do these things?

■ With young children, sing "This Is the Way I Brush My Teeth." Sing the song again, each time substituting a new skill:

This is the way I comb my hair....
This is the way I dress myself....

Ask the children to suggest additional verses. Talk about how much the children have already learned to do for themselves and how independent they are becoming.

■ Can you think of some things you can never do by yourself? Is that okay, too?

Develop children's language skills and continue the discussion of independence and self-reliance by weaving the following vocabulary words into your day.

by myself	freedom
choices	group
confidence	independence
decisions	interdependent
family	self-reliance

Things to Do in the Classroom

Activities for children of all ages

■ Provide opportunities for problem-solving and making choices. Encourage children to choose which learning centers they want to work in, which activities they want to do, which colors they want to paint with. When problems occur, such as juice spills or balls going into a water puddle, invite the children to think of solutions.

■ Let children do as much for themselves as possible. Provide materials for them to clean up their own spills. Keep art materials and supplies on a low shelf so they can get what they need themselves. Teach them to ask a friend to help put on their art smock.

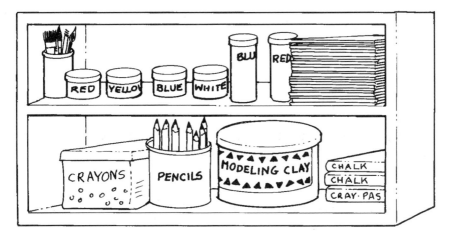

■ Young children need strong, supportive relationships with parents, caregivers and teachers in order to achieve independence. When they come to you for hugs and support, provide what is needed and then encourage them toward independent behaviors. Young children are in the process of developing the confidence they need for independent behavior. They periodically come to you for reinforcement and refueling and then need to be directed back into activities that build their self-sufficiency.

■ Discuss the interdependence of the members of the classroom. Compare the things children can do by themselves to the things that it takes everyone working together to achieve.

■ Use rebus directions in learning centers to encourage independent, self-directed work.

Independence & Self-Reliance  85

■ Do an "I Am Special" circle. Ask one child to sit in the center of the circle. Let each child tell one special thing about the child in the center.

■ Encourage games and activities that can be played alone. Some games traditionally played with a partner make good games to play against yourself.

DROP THE CLOTHESPIN IN THE BOTTLE—Encourage children to see if they can increase the number of pins in the bottle each time they play

TIDDLY-WINKS—Invite children to increase the number of chips in the cup each time they play.

BALANCE BEAM WALKING—Encourage children to try walking with a beanbag on their head, shoulder, knee and toe. (They'll have to hop with the beanbag on their knees and toes. Let them figure that out.) Encourage them to try going a little farther each time. (Create a "balance beam" with masking tape on the floor.)

■ Encourage children to develop independent skills.

WEAVING—Provide a variety of looms and encourage children to create unique weavings.

SCULPTING—Give the children playdough, clay and dough for sculpting.

■ Invite the children to celebrate their individuality and interdependence with a puzzle-piece mural. Cut a large sheet of mural paper into puzzle pieces (one piece for each child). Encourage children to paint or draw themselves or something about them on their puzzle piece. When everyone is finished, help the class put the puzzle together.

The Values Book

Working With Families: Ideas for Home

Activities for children of all ages

■ Help children be self-sufficient as soon as possible. Teach them to brush their own teeth, put on their shoes, pour their own juice, select clothes and dress themselves. Children are completely dependent at birth. Holding on to their dependent behaviors can become habit-forming for parents. We get so accustomed to taking care of every need that we forget to turn some of that responsibility over to children. It's also often easier to do it ourselves than to suffer through the tedious chore of letting them do it themselves. Pay attention to children's developmental levels and move them gradually into self-reliance.

■ Praise children's independence. When Julie puts on her shoes and socks, compliment her efforts. When Reed buttons his shirt, let him know how pleased and proud you are. You'll reinforce and encourage independent behaviors, and you'll give your children much-needed acceptance and attention. The more they get at home, the less likely they are to seek it outside.

■ Call attention to the interdependence of the family. It takes everyone working together to get out of the house and off to school and work in the morning. The work is easier if everyone helps prepare breakfast and clean up afterwards.

■ Encourage children to entertain themselves. There are several games, such as jacks and pick-up sticks, and activities, such as working puzzles and drawing, that one person can do alone.

■ Look at your child's baby book together. Point out how your child has grown more and more independent. Talk about first rolling over, first smiles, first steps and so on. Make a growth chart for your child. Use it to show new accomplishments and independent behaviors as well as height.

Activities for older children

■ Help children find their unique talents and encourage them to develop them. One child may play the violin, another might be good at gymnastics. One might be a natural artist, another might be great at jumping rope or riding a bike.

■ Take a camping trip. Let children experience taking care of themselves without the support and ease of community resources, such as electricity, running water, telephones and supermarkets.

Books to Share With Children

Read books that illustrate and encourage independence and self-reliance. Check your library for some of those listed here. Each one provides opportunities to discuss being independent.

ABC I Like Me by Nancy Carlson
All By Myself by Anna Grossnickle Hines
Argyle by Brooks B. Wallace
Bunny Cakes by Rosemary Wells
Little Big Girl by Althea Jane Horner
Mrs. Brice's Mice by Syd Hoff
The Story of Ferdinand by Munro Leaf
You're My Nikki by Phyllis Rose Eisenberg

Loyalty

Make new friends but keep the old,
One is silver and the other's gold.

*L*oyalty

What Is Loyalty?

We display loyalty when we remain faithfully committed to a person—a family member or friend—or to a particular group or cause we believe in. Loyalty implies maintaining that commitment through difficulties and despite obstacles.

Why Is Loyalty Important? Things for Adults to Think About

■ Loyalty is related to commitment. It is the character trait that allows us to stay faithful to our commitments and obligations.

Think of people, activities or causes to which you are committed. If loyalty were not part of the picture, would you still be committed?

■ Loyalty was one of the values that early Americans held in high esteem. You find many references to it in history—in the Constitution, the Pledge of Allegiance, stories of war heroes. During the Vietnam War there were many factors affecting loyalty. People on both sides of the issue felt that they were loyal.

Are loyalty and patriotism the same thing? How are they alike? How are they different?

■ Loyalty includes being loyal to one's self. Do people you know stand up for what they believe in? Do you? Are they easily persuaded by others to give up their point of view? Are you?

Think of something about which you feel strongly. How might you respond in the face of opposition?

■ Loyalty often requires sacrifice. In war time, the sacrifice may mean someone's life. In friendship, the sacrifice might mean giving up something you want to do in order to help a friend. In the workplace, it could mean quitting your job because the circumstances surrounding your job prohibit you from being loyal to your employer, and your sense of integrity prohibits your working for someone to whom you can't be loyal.

Think of some situations that have required your loyalty. Was a sacrifice made?

■ Sometimes loyalty requires a promise, such as an oath of office or marriage vow.

Make a list of recent promises you have made. How many have you kept?

Talking With Children About Loyalty

Is loyalty a value worth keeping? Talk with children about the ideas below and see what they think about loyalty.

■ Tell about a promise you have made. Did you keep it? How did keeping it or not keeping it make you feel?

■ Name some groups to which you belong such as your family, your class at school, or your neighborhood. What does it take to be loyal to these groups?

■ Think about a time when you gave up something you wanted to do in order to help a friend or a family member. How did you feel when you made the decision to give up your plans? How did you feel after you helped your friend?

■ Sing "Make New Friends." Ask the children to explain the ways in which both new and old friends are valuable. Explain the analogies in the song to silver and gold.

Develop children's language skills and continue the discussion of loyalty by weaving the following vocabulary words into your day.

beliefs	friends
cause	loyalty
commitment	promise
faithful	sacrifice
family	trust

Things to Do in the Classroom

Activities for children of all ages

■ Teach a unit on friends and family. Work the concept of loyalty into the activities. For example, invite the children to brainstorm a list of ways family members are loyal to each other.

■ Discuss ways children can be loyal to their school, such as keeping it clean and participating in school activities.

The Values Book

■ Help children be faithful to their own thinking. When casting a vote or choosing an activity or even a color of paint for their painting, encourage children to do their own thinking. Children frequently wait to see what their peers do before choosing a course of action. Sometimes this is merely a result of not having enough information. Be sure children have enough information to make their own decisions.

■ Reward independent thinking. Encourage activities that allow diversity, and reduce the number of activities that are convergent in nature. Help children appreciate the feelings that accompany sticking to your own point of view. For example, after you read "The Little Red Hen," ask the children whether they think it is okay that the Little Red Hen chose not to share her bread. Ask children to explain and justify their answers. Accept and respect all answers that can be justified. Celebrate the diversity of answers; encourage children to feel good about their individual responses.

Activities for older children

■ Play team games. You might want to challenge another group of children to a relay race or game of kick ball. Children need to experience both competitive and noncompetitive games. Competition encourages children to stretch themselves; noncompetitive games help children develop a sense of cooperation and play.

■ Present the children with the following scenario: You've promised your best friend you would come over after school. In the meantime, your next-door neighbor invites you to a birthday party at the local amusement park. What do you do? Encourage discussion.

Loyalty

■ Let children choose a cause they're interested in, such as fire safety, seat belt safety or recycling. Invite them to organize an awareness-raising campaign, including making bumper stickers.

Don't play with matches!

Plan an escape route.

Check your fire alarm.

Working With Families: Ideas for Home

Activities for children of all ages

■ Discuss ways your family members are loyal to each other, such as standing up for each other, supporting each other's accomplishments and efforts and helping each other when needed.

■ Make up a family pledge, slogan or cheer, such as "In the Smith family, it's all for one and one for all."

 The Values Book

■ Respect your child's right to have ideas that are different from your own. Children must be loyal to themselves before they can learn to be loyal to others.

■ Help children understand that when they give their word on something like staying in their own yard or having their room straight before dinner, they are, in essence, making a promise. Keeping that promise means staying loyal to their word.

Activities for older children

■ Encouraging your children to participate in groups and activities helps promote their sense of loyalty. Try a Summer reading program at your local library, or contact the Blue Birds or the Ranger Rick Club.

■ Does your family have a coat of arms? Research it and share its meaning with your children. How many attributes illustrated on the coat of arms do you still uphold in your family today? Design your own coat of arms with values that are important to your family.

Books to Share With Children

Read books that illustrate and encourage loyalty. Check your library for some of those listed here. Each one provides opportunities to discuss loyalty and faithfulness.

Amos and Boris by William Steig
Best Friends by Steven Kellogg
Big Brother Dustin by Alden R. Carter
Chester's Way by Kevin Henkes
Frog and Toad Are Friends by Arnold Lobel
Mama Do You Love Me? by Barbara Joosse
Mama Provi and the Pot of Rice by Sylvia Rosa-Casanova
Matthew and Tilly by Rebecca Jones
My Love for You by Susan L. Roth
The Velveteen Rabbit by Margery Williams

Patience

She'll be comin' 'round the mountain when she comes!
She'll be comin' 'round the mountain when she comes!
She'll be comin' 'round the mountain,
She'll be comin' 'round the mountain,
She'll be comin' 'round the mountain when she comes!

Patience

What Is Patience?

Many of us have a tendency

toward immediate

gratification—we want what we

want right now. We exhibit

patience when we are able to

handle delays en route to a goal

or special occasion and to

endure the wait calmly.

The Values Book

Why Is Patience Important? Things for Adults to Think About

■ Our hurry-up society doesn't offer children very many opportunities to learn how to be patient. Microwaves turn out hot dogs in thirty seconds. Charge cards allow parents to provide children with bicycles or new wardrobes for school the moment they need or want them. We can even obtain a suntan in less than twenty minutes in a tanning booth.

Brainstorm a list of things you can get in a hurry that you used to have to wait for.

■ Remember waiting all day for a pot of beans to cook, or putting a much desired item in layaway and using your weekly allowance to pay for it? Both of these experiences and many others taught us patience and also helped us develop a sense of satisfaction and pride.

Think of something you bought on layaway. Do you remember what it felt like when you made the last payment?

■ Part of the fun of wanting something is the planning of how to get it. The small steps we take toward fulfilling our goal are celebrations within themselves. We do children a disservice by not finding opportunities for them to learn the joy of waiting.

List three things that are small steps, or celebrations, leading up to a special holiday, birthday or anniversary.

Talking With Children About Patience

Is patience a value worth keeping? Talk with children about the ideas below and see what they think about patience.

■ Brainstorm a list of things that are hard to wait for. Make a list of suggestions of things you could do to make the waiting easier.

■ Think about something that took you a long time to learn, such as whistling, learning to pour or tying your shoes. Now that you've accomplished your goal, do you think it was worth the wait?

■ With young children, sing "She'll Be Comin' 'Round the Mountain." Ask the children to describe what's happening in the song. Explain that the song illustrates waiting and patiently anticipating a special occasion.

■ Think of something that you want and make a plan to get it.

Develop children's language skills and continue the discussion of patience by weaving the following vocabulary words into your day.

anticipation	now
calm	patience
delay	planning
goal	preparation
later	waiting

Things to Do in the Classroom

Activities for all ages

■ Work on arts and crafts projects that take time to complete. Talk to children about the fun of watching the project develop. Review with the children the steps they have completed and plan together for the next steps.

■ Plan a class play. Let children decide on the play, make costumes and props, create an invitation to invite another class, and finally, perform the play. Help children see each step of getting ready as a satisfying activity.

The Values Book

■ Grow a garden. As children watch the seeds sprout, encourage them to enjoy the daily changes. You might want to provide a magnifying glass to observe small changes, or use a popsicle stick to measure weekly growth. Make vegetable soup with your crop. Or, if you can't grow a garden, just make vegetable soup. Involve the children in all the steps: buying the vegetables at the store (or bringing them from home), washing the vegetables, cutting them up, putting them in the pot, adding seasoning and bouillon, waiting while they cook, then finally, enjoying the tasty soup together. It was worth the wait! (See page 42 for a soup recipe.)

■ Talk to children about waiting for important events, such as birthdays or exciting field trips. Let them brainstorm the small, fun things leading up to the event, such as picking out a gift, talking to their families about the event or deciding what they will wear.

■ Do a cooking project that requires waiting. Make popsicles, bake yeast bread (see bread recipe, page 43) or make cookies from a dough that has to chill overnight.

Frozen Color Pops

1/2 cup (125 ml) orange juice
3 ounces (90 g) fresh raspberries or strawberries
1 teaspoon (5 ml) sugar

1/4 cup (60 ml) water
1/4 cup (60 ml) grape juice
1/4 cup (60 ml) cold water

4 small paper cups
blender

strainer
measuring cups

ice-cream or craft sticks

1. Pour about 1 inch (2.5 cm) of orange juice into each paper cup.
2. Place the cups in the freezer for about 2 hours.
3. Place the raspberries or strawberries, sugar and water into the blender and process until smooth.
4. Pour this berry mixture through a strainer. Set aside.
5. Remove the frozen orange juice from the freezer. Pour the strained berry mixture over the frozen orange juice.
6. Return the frozen juices to the freezer for about 1 hour, until almost frozen.
7. Mix grape juice with 1/4 cup cold water. Set aside.
8. Remove the frozen orange juice and berry mixture from the freezer. Pour the grape juice mixture over strawberry or raspberry layer. Insert ice-cream sticks or craft sticks and freeze the mixture overnight.
9. Take the fruit pops out of the freezer and let sit for a few seconds, then grasp by the handles and pull out of the cups.

Reprinted from COOKING ART by MaryAnn Kohl and Jean Potter
(Gryphon House, 1997)

Gingerbread Cookies

1/2 cup (125 ml) shortening
1/2 cup (125 ml) molasses
1/2 cup (100 g) sugar
1/4 cup (60 ml) water
2 1/2 cups (500 g) flour

3/4 teaspoon (3.5 ml) salt
1/2 teaspoon (2.5 ml) baking soda
3/4 teaspoon (3.5 ml) ginger
1/4 teaspoon (1 ml) nutmeg
1/8 teaspoon (.5 ml) all-spice

measuring cups and spoons
mixing bowl and spoon
rolling pin and plastic wrap
wooden board or clean table top

cookie cutters
cookie sheet
oven or toaster oven

1. Place all ingredients in the mixing bowl and mix well.
2. Chill the dough for 2-3 hours or overnight.
3. Place the dough on a floured board and roll it out.
4. Using cookie cutters (could be people or any other shape), cut out the cookies.
5. Decorate cookies, if desired, with raisins, chocolate chips or sprinkles.
6. Place on a cookie sheet and bake at 375°F (190°C) for 10-12 minutes.

Reprinted from *THE GIANT ENCYCLOPEDIA OF THEME ACTIVITIES FOR CHILDREN 2 TO 5* (Gryphon House, 1993)

Activities for older children

■ Read chapter books. Nothing builds patience better than having to wait to find out what happens. Help children learn to discuss the book with their friends. Help them learn how to speculate and predict. Try one of the books listed below or ask your librarian for other suggestions.

Charlotte's Web by E.B. White
The Five Hundred Hats of Bartholomew Cubbins by
   Dr. Seuss
Mr. Popper's Penguins by
   Richard and Florence
   Atwater
Pippi Longstocking by
   Astrid Lindgren
Ramona the Pest by
   Beverly Cleary

The Values Book

■ Invite the children to choose an item (for example, a game or a set of blocks) they would like to have in the classroom. Encourage them to plan money-making projects to fund their purchase. Talk about the steps the children go through to reach their goal. Make sure the purchase is made by mid-year so that the children have plenty of time to enjoy what they buy.

Working With Families: Ideas for Home

Activities for children of all ages

■ Set up an allowance system for children. Help them figure out how to save money toward a special toy or activity. If you can find a store that accepts layaway, use it.

■ Cook with children. Bake bread, make soup or mix up a cookie dough that requires overnight chilling (see pages 42, 43, 101 and 102 for recipes to try). Help children celebrate the steps toward completion.

■ Let children help with a project that takes time to complete, like refinishing a piece of furniture, crocheting a blanket or redoing a bedroom.

■ Plan a trip. Look at a map to help choose a destination, send off for brochures, plan and save for expenses, decide on a wardrobe, make arrangements for care of the house in your absence. Make a timeline showing when different aspects of the trip must be set in motion (for example, deposits on hotels and packing of suitcases).

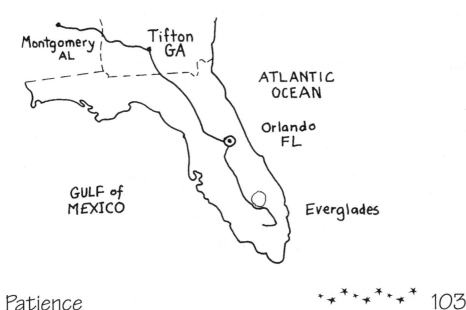

■ Read a book together as a family, perhaps every night after dinner or at bedtime. Discuss the book with each other. Help children learn to speculate and enjoy guessing about the plot with each other.

■ Keep a family scrapbook. Take it out from time to time and look at it together. Help children develop an appreciation for the passing of time. One of the best ways to do this is to let them look at their own pictures and talk about how they've changed.

■ Let children make old-fashioned Valentines—the kind with lots of glue, paper doilies and special decorations. This project should take several days as children come back and evaluate their progress and decide what another layer of glue and decorations might add. (This is not just for Valentines. Send homemade thank you notes or "I Love You" cards or "Have a Good Week" cards.)

Activities for older children

■ Work jigsaw puzzles together. Choose a spot in the house where the puzzle can stay out for a while. The project is sure to last for at least a couple of weeks and it's sure to bring a sense of satisfaction when completed.

■ Play a game of Monopoly that continues over time. Keep the board in a safe place. How long can you keep the game going?

■ Find a local store that will allow your child to buy something on the layaway plan.

Books to Share With Children

Read books that illustrate and encourage patience. Check your library for some of those listed here. Each one provides opportunities to talk about patience, anticipation, planning and/or preparing.

The Carrot Seed by Ruth Krauss
Dance, Tanya by Patricia Gauch
Dear Daddy by John Schindel
The Growing-Up Feet by Beverly Cleary
I Can't Wait by Elizabeth Crary
I Need a Lunch Box by Jeannette Caines
Lilly's Purple Plastic Purse by Kevin Henkes
Not Yet, Yvette by Helen Ketteman
Pablo's Tree by Pat Mora
Something Is Going to Happen by Charlotte Zolotow
The Whale's Song by Dyan Sheldon

Pride

A B C D E F G
H I J K L M N O P
Q R S T U V
W X Y and Z.
Now I've said my ABCs.
Won't you say you're proud of me?

ride

What Is Pride?

Pride is the sense we have of

our own genuine self-worth. It is

self-respect. Pride is also the

special pleasure we feel when

we accomplish a

challenging task, achieve a

difficult goal, or even acquire

a particular possession.

Why Is Pride Important? Things for Adults to Think About

■ Many events contributed to the collective image Americans have held of themselves as being proud—the struggle and endurance of the early pioneers and settlers, the triumph of winning independence from England, the glory of defeating totalitarianism in World War I and World War II, surviving the Depression, working to establish The Great Society and maintaining a position among other countries as world leader. All of these events are perceived by the majority of American people as right and just efforts, worthy of pride.

In the early 1900s when the population of the United States grew with the influx of immigrants, the sense of pride at being an American grew, as well. Immigrants were proud and grateful to be part of America.

If your family immigrated to the United States, when did they come? Where did your family come from? Why did they come here? Can you remember hearing your parents or grandparents talk about any of the events mentioned above? Which events did they express pride in? What other events have you heard people talk about with pride?

■ Since the 1960s and 70s, we have experienced expanded news coverage. American imperfections and failings like Vietnam, Watergate and Civil Rights injustices were brought into our living rooms. Our collective image of a proud people and a great nation was forever changed.

Does pride have to be earned, and if so, have we fallen short of the earning? Watch the news tonight. On a piece of paper, make a check mark for each story that makes you feel proud. Mark an X for each story that makes you feel bad, embarrassed or ashamed.

■ Pride is associated with struggle. What comes easy for us, we take for granted. What we struggle to obtain often results in a sense of satisfaction that leads to a sense of pride.

What was your last struggle? Did it leave you feeling proud?

■ Pride often fuels motivation. Being proud of our work encourages us to be productive and to strive for quality. Team pride often drives competition. Self-pride is often at the heart of the decisions we make.

Pride

What decisions do people make based on pride? For example, accepting or not accepting help from someone, refusing to admit mistakes or indiscretions, choosing a line of work and so on.

■ Pride has many aspects. When balanced with temperance, we feel happy, gratified and content. When we have an abundance of pride, we can be boastful, arrogant and conceited.

Think of people you know in each category. Which category do you fit into? Have you always been in that category? What is different now?

■ Being proud of yourself contributes to positive self-esteem.

Make a list of the personal characteristics you are proud of.

■ The practice of other virtues can foster pride. When we stick to our commitments, we generally build a sense of pride. As we exercise patience, tolerance and empathy, we feel proud of our efforts.

Think of a commitment you are keeping. Do you feel proud? When was the last time you exercised patience? How did you feel afterwards?

Talking With Children About Pride

Is pride a value worth keeping? Discuss the following questions with children and see what they think about pride.

■ Have you done something that you're proud of? Did you have to work at it, practice it, struggle before you could achieve it? What else about yourself are you proud of? Is it something that you inherited? Is it something that other people hold in high regard?

■ Think of something you've had to struggle to achieve, like riding a bicycle, blowing a bubble or whistling. Why did you feel proud when you were able to accomplish the task?

■ With young children, sing the alphabet song. Encourage them to remember how they felt when they finally mastered the alphabet. Ask older children to name some of the challenges they are working to meet now.

The Values Book

■ Do you belong to any group that you feel pleased or proud to be a part of? Why are you pleased?

■ Having too much pride in our accomplishments or our possessions can make us conceited, arrogant and difficult to be around, like Lucy in the *Charlie Brown* cartoons, Angelica in the *Rugrats* cartoons and Cera in *Land Before Time*. Can you think of someone who shows too much pride? Have you ever been too proud?

Develop children's language skills and continue the discussion of pride by weaving the following vocabulary words into your day.

accomplishment	goal
achievement	motivation
challenge	practice
commitment	pride
effort	struggle

Things to Do in the Classroom

Activities for children of all ages

■ Do a project that will challenge the children. For example, invite the children to try different types of weaving. Provide 2" (5 cm) strips of paper for place mat weaving. String four strips of elastic across a Styrofoam meat tray and invite children to weave ribbons and lace through it. Provide looms and fabric rings for weaving potholders. After children have accomplished the tasks, discuss the difference between easy and difficult.

■ Encourage children always to do the best they can in everything they do. Discuss how our efforts and the quality of our work are often seen as a reflection of ourselves.

■ Encourage children to describe the steps taken to complete projects. Point out that in order to be proud of our work, we may have to exercise patience and we may have to make a commitment to finish before we even begin.

■ Pride can be both a motivator and a companion to other virtues discussed in this book. As you do some of the activities in other chapters, assess whether pride is involved as a motivating force, a companion or both.

Pride  111

■ Have children think about the things they know how to do (for example, draw a picture, build a road, ride a bicycle, tie shoes, read). Ask them how many times they failed before they succeeded. Teach them to say "I practiced" instead of "I failed" or "I couldn't."

Activities for older children

■ Encourage children to get involved in a community service project they can take pride in. You might start by sharing stories of other children and their projects. Check your library for one of the books listed below.

Kids Making Quilts for Kids by ABC Quilts
The Helping Hands Handbook by P. Adams and J. Marzollo
A Kids' Guide to How to Save the Planet by B. Goodman
No Kidding Around! America's Young Activists Are Changing the World and You Can, Too! by W. Lesko

■ Help the children write a class song. Maybe they want to use "Hey, Look Me Over" as an inspiration for ideas. Sing their new song to familiar melodies, such as "Row, Row, Row Your Boat" or "Here We Go 'Round the Mulberry Bush." Children may also enjoy designing a class banner.

  The Values Book

Working With Families: Ideas for Home

Activities for children of all ages

■ Use praise appropriately. Be specific, focus on improvement of process rather than evaluation of a finished product. Avoid comparisons and competition. Use direct comments delivered in a natural voice. "Steve, I like the way you included Corinne in the game."

■ Share your own accomplishments and ideas. Show your pride. Discuss your thinking along the way. Did you consciously think, "How can I make this better?"

■ When a movie you watch with your child has a theme of pride, use it as a springboard for discussion. *The Lion King* is a good example. Simba was filled with false pride until tragedy made him reassess his situation. He eventually learned that respect has to be earned.

■ Be careful in selecting which of your children's accomplishments you express pride in. For example, showing pride in your child winning beauty pageants or games may send the wrong message to young children. They may internalize the idea that self-worth is based on superficial criteria instead of on intangible qualities such as kindness, commitment, intelligence and cooperation.

■ Try this activity during dinner. Go around the table and ask each person to complete this sentence: "I am proud of myself for____" or "I am proud of ___ for ___."

■ As a family, make a totem that illustrates your family pride. Use empty oatmeal boxes or coffee cans. Using colored paper, fabric scraps, odds and ends and natural objects, decorate each one to show something about your family. Include such things as heritage, language and values you hold dear, such as kindness, honesty, fairness and responsibility.

■ Help children to use positive self-talk. For example, "the children don't know me" instead of "the children don't like me." Our sense of self-pride can be enhanced and diminished by the things we say to ourselves.

■ Affirm children's success by attributing it to their efforts or other things over which they have control.

■ When your child approaches an important time or event, such as starting school, do something to make the occasion special and memorable. Show your pride in your child.

Books to Share With Children

Read books that illustrate and encourage pride. Check your library for some of those listed here. Each one provides opportunities to discuss appropriate, healthy pride or inappropriate pride and boastfulness.

Annabelle Swift, Kindergartner by Amy Schwartz
The Emperor's New Clothes by Hans Christian Andersen
Gina by Bernard Waber
The Gingerbread Boy by Paul Galdone
I Am Better Than You! by Robert Lopshire
My Head Is Full of Colors by Catherine Friend
Pepita Talks Twice by Ofelia Dumas Lachtman
Roxaboxen by Alice McLerran

Resourcefulness

There's a hole in my bucket, dear Liza, dear Liza.
There's a hole in my bucket, dear Liza, a hole.

Then mend it, dear Johnny, dear Johnny, dear Johnny.
Then mend it, dear Johnny, dear Johnny, mend it.

With what shall I mend it, dear Liza, dear Liza?
With what shall I mend it, dear Liza, mend it?

With a straw, dear Johnny, dear Johnny, dear Johnny.
With a straw, dear Johnny, dear Johnny, a straw. . . .

Resourcefulness

What Is Resourcefulness?

Resourcefulness is our ability to think creatively of different methods and materials for handling new or difficult situations. Resourcefulness allows us to consider, using our imagination, all possible options in finding a solution to a problem.

Why Is Resourcefulness Important? Things for Adults to Think About

■ Resourcefulness was a necessary tool for early settlers and pioneers as they established communities and homes in a new land that was often without the resources they may have had in their homelands.

Native Americans had to be resourceful as they were forced to move from their homes to new land that called for different survival skills. For example, tribes that had survived as hunters were called on to learn new skills like farming and weaving. Being receptive to learning new skills in times of crisis is one form of resourcefulness.

When you were a child and had to learn something new, how did you feel? Threatened? Eager? Inadequate? Capable? As an adult, how do you feel about learning something new?

■ Our nation's prosperity, being in the land of plenty, has created an attitude of taking things—materials and natural resources—for granted and has allowed, maybe even encouraged, us to become a throw-away society. In times past, when a piece of furniture broke it was fixed, not discarded as often happens today. Sometimes we forget—or neglect—to try thinking of new ways to use old things.

Is it possible that the more we have the less we have to exercise our resourcefulness? Is true resourcefulness a respect for resources?

■ For the past several decades, our schools have focused on curriculum that teaches convergent thinking and rote memorization. Children are given little or no opportunity to practice problem-solving skills or individual thinking. With each subject relegated to a specific time slot, children are not encouraged to transfer information and skills learned in one area of the curriculum to another.

Describe your most memorable teacher. What methods of teaching did he or she use? Why does that teacher stand out in your mind?

■ The Electronic Age offers an abundance of equipment that basically solves problems for us. Many activities that once required and allowed practice of problem-solving skills now happen electronically with the push of a few buttons.

When was the last time you raised the hood of your car to listen to and diagnose a problem there? When was the last time you spent hours at the library, poring over volumes of books for some specific information. Can you think of tasks and problems people took care of in the past that are now handled by computers? Is this always a good thing?

■ It is often resourcefulness that is at the heart of great discoveries. The Post-it Note is a good example. The initial goal at 3M was to develop a super stick glue. Instead of discarding the glue that failed, someone found a good use for it. What a discovery! Resourcefulness can take the form of creativity in the midst of failure.

Describe a recent failure. Did you try again? What happened? What resources did you use?

■ It is often resourcefulness that turns disaster to opportunity. Merck worked five years to find a medicine that would cure a blindness occurring in developing countries. They developed an appropriate medicine but were unable to sell it to a philanthropic group as they had planned. Instead of ditching the medicine, which would have been a terrible waste, they gave it to the people who needed it. They even developed channels of distribution at the company's expense. This decision resulted in a major boost in morale for the company, widespread positive publicity and an increase in stock value. Resourcefulness can take the form of opportunity in the midst of disaster.

Have you turned a seeming disaster into a golden opportunity? What did you do?

■ Assess your problem-solving skills. Do you start to work on a problem immediately or do you take time to reflect? Does it matter how long you take or is it just a matter of eventually getting the problem solved? Are you good at solving problems? How does finding a solution make you feel?

Think of a problem that you have recently solved. Use it to assess your skills and individual style.

The Values Book

Talking With Children About Resourcefulness

Is resourcefulness a value worth keeping? Talk with children about the questions below and see what they think about resourcefulness.

■ How do you feel when you come up with a solution to a problem? Think of a problem you have overcome such as not having enough of something (maybe blocks to finish a building) or trying to reach something just beyond your grasp. What did you do? How did you feel when you encountered the problem? How did you feel after you found a solution?

■ When you have a problem, do you start thinking of ways to solve it right away? Do you take time to think? Do you ask for help? What steps do you take? How we attack a problem differs with individual preferences and with the situation. What matters is that we act and that we act in a way that improves the situation.

■ Sing "Dear Liza" with your children. Talk about the way the characters in the song first identify the problems and then think creatively to find solutions.

■ With older children, ask them how they make decisions. Do they take the easy way—what's quick and painless? Do they make a list of pros and cons? Do they follow the crowd? Ask them to think about a recent decision they made. Would they make the same decision now? Why? Why not?

Develop children's language skills and continue the discussion of resourcefulness by weaving the following vocabulary words into your day.

creativity	problems
imagination	resources
ingenuity	resourcefulness
materials	solutions
opportunity	useful

Things to Do in the Classroom

Activities for children of all ages

■ Change materials in learning centers regularly. Encourage exploration. Ask children to look around the room for objects and materials that have more than one use (e.g., straws for drinking, straws for blowing paint, cut-up straws for stringing, etc.). Encourage children to use materials in new ways.

■ Encourage independence. Invite children to find ways they can help each other put on their painting smocks or settle a problem in the block center.

■ Play What If? Present situations and problems for children to think about and respond to. For example, "What would happen if their were no highways?" or "How would the world be different if the color blue did not exist?"

■ Set up a recycling center for classroom materials. Have children make a list of reasons to recycle materials.

■ Play What Is It? Hold up different objects/materials for children to examine. How many different uses can they come up with for each one? Children will come up with familiar uses quickly. Give them plenty of time afterwards to think about and express other options. For example, children may say that clothespins can be used to close a chip bag, hold a sponge or make an animal. If you wait out the period of incubation, you may hear additional ideas such as "to hold a nail while you hammer it."

*★ *★ *★ *★ *

■ A variation of the previous activity would be to present objects that have more than one use. For example, pencils come in a variety of shapes and sizes and are used in a variety of ways—drawing pencil, drafting pencil, fat pencil, colored pencil, eye pencil and so on. Talk about how the pencils are used. What things can you do with them? How do changes in design make pencils more useful?

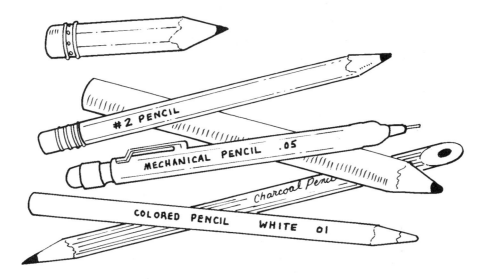

■ Set up problems for the children to solve. For example, when you get near the bottom of a big bag of chips, can they think of a way to make it easier to get to the chips on the bottom?

■ Offer choices in daily classroom activities as often as possible. Children need practice weighing the pros and cons of different options.

■ Involve children in decision-making opportunities. Perhaps the decision is where to go on a field trip, which kind of pet to get for the classroom or how to choose daily helpers.

Working With Families: Ideas for Home

Activities for children of all ages

■ Let your children solve their own problems. Consistently bailing them out encourages dependency and prohibits practicing resourcefulness.

Resourcefulness  121

■ Encourage independence. Teach your children to put on their socks and shoes as soon as they are able, invite them to help select their clothes each day, allow them to pour their own juice, choose their own bedtime story and make their own decisions when choices are offered.

■ Encourage exploration and trial and error. Children learn as much, possibly more, from their mistakes as they do from their successes.

■ Model problem-solving. Talk about your day, sharing problems and new situations you were faced with and how you responded. For example, your computer may have gone down in the middle of a rush assignment, you may have arrived at work this morning to find you have a new boss, perhaps you had to deal with a rude customer, or maybe you needed something that was out of stock.

■ When your children face a problem or new situation, help them consider pros and cons, ask questions and consider consequences of various responses. Demonstrate the process used to solve problems—think of possible solutions, choose one, try it out, evaluate the results. Help your children internalize this process.

■ Keep a box for discarded items like milk jugs, bicycle and wagon wheels, large sheets of cardboard, old clocks or nonworking appliances. Work with your child to build something new with the items.

The Values Book

■ Television shows are often centered around solving a specific problem. Although the problem generally gets solved, the method of solving the problem, or the thinking required, is often not visible to children. Discuss these shows with children and help them see the process of solution.

■ Many fictional characters, such as Pippi Longstocking, model resourcefulness in a way that's highly visible to children. Use stories and videos as springboards for discussion.

■ When children are faced with a decision, teach them how to weigh the pros and cons. Have them make a list and then go back over the list and place a check mark by the important items on each list. For example, children may be trying to decide whether to spend their allowance on a fish or a game. Many factors will contribute to the list of pros and cons, including cost, use, longevity, care required and fun expected.

Fish

Pros
1. Can watch it swim every day!
2. Will last a long time.
3. Costs $4.00

Cons
1. Need to feed it every day.
2. Food costs $1.00/week

Game

Pros
1. All the kids like it.
2. Will last a long time.

Cons
Costs $18.00.

Books to Share With Children

Read books that illustrate and encourage resourcefulness. Check your library for some of those listed here. Each one provides opportunities to discuss resourcefulness, problem-solving skills and ingenuity.

All Stuck Up by Linda Hayward
The Cat in the Hat by Dr. Seuss
The Cat in the Hat Comes Back by Dr. Seuss
Changes, Changes by Pat Hutchins
Chicken Sunday by Patricia Polacco
The Doorbell Rang by Pat Hutchins
A House for Hermit Crab by Eric Carle
How to Make an Apple Pie and See the World by Marjorie Priceman
Jennie's Hat by Ezra Jack Keats
Peter's Chair by Ezra Jack Keats
Snow Angel by Jean Marzollo
Something Special by Nicola Moon
Space Travellers by Margaret Wild

Respect

I love the flowers, I love the daffodils,
I love the mountains, I love the rolling hills,
I love the fireside, when all the lights are low,
Boom-de-a-da, boom-de-a-da,
Boom-de-a-da, boom-de-a-da.

Respect

What Is Respect?

We respect people when we

admire, appreciate and hold

them in particularly high esteem.

When we are polite to others

and treat them with courtesy,

we are showing respect.

Why Is Respect Important? Things for Adults to Think About

■ Our respect for individuals can have a profound effect on us. The people we admire often serve as models for how we shape our own lives. Who and what we respect plays a significant role in who we are. How many artists have followed the lead of Georgia O'Keeffe, Pablo Picasso and Leonardo DaVinci? How many peacemakers have emulated the work of Gandhi?

Think of people you respected when you were growing up. Did they serve as role models for you? Can you see characteristics, behaviors and attitudes in yourself that were modeled after those you held in esteem?

■ Does respect have to be earned or is it a given in some situations? Is it awarded individually or can it be obtained simply through membership in a certain group?

Many of us were taught to respect our elders, simply by virtue of their age. Is this still true today? Should it be? Most of us grew up with parents who respected the President of the United States and other authority figures just by virtue of their position. This is not as true today. What do you think?

■ Have we moved from being a society that collectively agreed on who and what deserved our respect to one that is more focused on individual determination? Have we moved from being a society that automatically grants respect to one that grants respect only to those who earn it? On what criteria should respect be based?

What things do you respect? Who are some of the people you respect? What is it about them that you admire? Has the media affected your choices? If so, how?

■ There are different types of respect—acceptance, regard, admiration, appreciation, honor.

Think of an example for each category of respect.

■ Are we satisfied to be a culture that, in general, unconditionally admires or respects people for their star status? Do we want to instill in our children a more thoughtful determination of who deserves their admiration and respect?

Make a list of criteria for establishing respect.

■ Should our laws (for example, stopping for red lights, respecting property rights, etc.) be decided through a collective effort? Should the rules be accepted unconditionally?

Think of an instance when disregard for or disobedience of a law might be justified. What do you think is the most effective way of establishing and maintaining a fair and just body of law?

■ Henry David Thoreau wrote, "The earth is more to be admired than to be used." Promoting respect and care for the environment is an important issue today.

Do you agree with Thoreau? What does it mean to admire or respect the earth? How do you show your respect for it?

Talking With Children About Respect

Is respect a value worth keeping? Talk with children about the questions below and see what they think about respect.

■ Ask children what respect means to them. They may not have a definition, but they may be able to provide an example.

■ Ask children to tell who and what they respect or admire and why.

■ Sing "I Love the Flowers" with the children. Help them to see that our enjoyment of the beautiful things in nature is tied to respect—we appreciate nature so we want to take care of it.

■ Discuss respect for rules, such as not hurting others and not destroying someone else's property. Help children understand that respecting rules is a way of respecting people. Respect protects our own rights as well as the rights of others.

The Values Book

Develop children's language skills and continue the discussion of respect by weaving the following vocabulary words into your day.

acceptance	polite
admire	preserve
appreciate	protect
courtesy	respect
honor	self-respect

Things to Do in the Classroom

Activities for children of all ages

■ One of the best ways for children to internalize the concept of respect is to be treated with respect. Allow them to be partners in their learning. Encourage them to make suggestions, and value their ideas by including their suggestions in your plans. Listen when they speak and answer their questions seriously.

■ Provide lessons and activities that teach respect. Lessons about self can enhance self-esteem and promote self-respect. Ecology and animal lessons can emphasize respect for the environment and for living things. Lessons about families and friends can encourage respect for other people.

Self—*Encourage children to create paper chains of respect. Invite them to decorate strips of paper to show ways they respect and take care of themselves. Glue the strips into loops to make a chain.*

Ecology—*Invite children to meet a tree and listen to its "heartbeat." Spring is the best time to do this. Choose a tree at least six inches in diameter and preferably with a thin bark. Give the children a stethoscope and encourage them to hold it against the tree to hear the "life" rushing through, just like the blood through our bodies.*

Family and Friends—*Brainstorm a list of ways family members and friends respect and care for each other. Talk about how family members work together to take care of the family.*

Animals—Take a field trip to a working farm. Talk about ways that animals take care of us. For example, they give us milk, they help us work, they take us places, they give us eggs and meat, they give us wool and so on. How do we take care of animals?

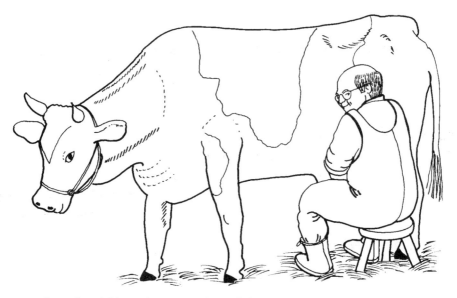

■ Talk to the children about people and things you respect. Be sure to emphasize how you decide who and what you respect. Do the people you respect have common characteristics? What about the ideas and institutions you respect?

■ When children express admiration for super heroes (or any character), discuss their feelings with them. Is their admiration justified? Do they admire or look up to someone or something just because their friends do? What is special or admirable about the character that they admire?

■ Encourage children to practice showing respect by using a talking stick during circle or group discussions. Provide a dowel about one foot long. Invite children to decorate it with paints, feathers, yarn, ribbons and other materials. Pass the stick around the circle. Whoever is holding the stick has the floor and the others listen attentively.

■ Invite senior citizens to participate in class activities. The interaction will encourage the development of respect in both directions.

The Values Book

■ Encourage the children to create character webs for story characters. After reading or telling a story, write the name of the main character on chart paper. Ask the children to describe the character's personality and actions. Does the character have traits we can admire? What are they? Would children like to be like the character?

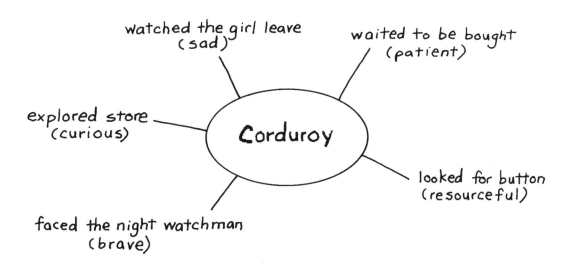

Working With Families: Ideas for Home

Activities for children of all ages

■ Respect your children. Listen to their ideas, try their suggestions, include them in conversations, afford them the benefit of the doubt, give them choices, speak to them at their eye level, honor their efforts. If you have to tell them "no," be sure you explain why. If you are making a family plan for a trip or an event, be sure to include them in the planning.

■ Model respect for laws. Don't break a law or rule, then expect your child to honor it. For example, don't bring a towel home from the hotel you stayed in during your business trip and then expect your child to refrain from stealing.

■ Talk about people you respect. Point out character traits that you admire (for example, honesty, kindness, responsibility, etc.) in each person.

■ Help your children use good critical judgment when they select heroes. Ask questions that test their judgment. For example, "What do you like about ____? How is ____ like ____? How are they different?"

■ Help your children understand that respect for property is an extension of respect for the owner. Begin by respecting their property. Knock before you go into your child's room. Don't assume that it's okay to donate last year's stuffed toy to Goodwill. Your child may still be attached to it. Don't open your children's mail unless they ask for help. Encourage them to treat other people's things with respect as well.

■ Give your children plenty of positive attention. As parents, we sometimes fall into a trap of watching our children so that we can "catch" them at something. Flip that around. Try to catch them doing something kind, caring, friendly and so on. Show your respect for them. Let them know this is the kind of behavior that you expect.

■ Most of us have heard and said things like "You're just like your dad" or "Your Aunt Karen always loved cats, too." Talk about characteristics and behaviors your children have in common with other family members. Lead them to see that we can choose the people and behaviors that we will model our own after. Expose them to good role models.

■ Take your child on a walk through a park. Stop and hug a tree. Notice the flowers, the grass, the shrubbery. Talk about ways that people and plants take care of each other. What can you do to take better care of the earth?

■ Visit a zoo, a farm or a pet store. Talk about ways that animals take care of us. For example, they love us and keep us company, they give us milk, they give us wool, and so on. How do we take care of animals?

■ Be careful what you say. Many of us use slang expressions without even thinking about what they might mean. Have you ever called someone an "Indian giver"? A "redneck"? Have you heard or used the phrase "Jew down"? Pay attention to what you say and to what your children say. Talk about how words can be disrespectful and hurtful to others.

Books to Share With Children

Read books that illustrate and encourage respect. Check your library for some of those listed here. Each one provides opportunities to discuss respect.

Alejandro's Gift by Richard Albert
Alexander and the Terrible, Horrible, No Good, Very Bad Day by Judith Viorst
Dear Mr. Blueberry by Simon James
Elijah's Angel: A Story for Chanukah and Christmas by Michael J. Rosen
Gina by Bernard Waber
Hey! Get Off Our Train! by John Burningham
Hooray for Me! by Remy Charlip and Lilian Moore
Island Baby by Holly Keller
Milo and the Magical Stones by Marcus Pfister
Owl Moon by Jane Yolen
Rockabye Crocodile by José Aruego

Responsibility

Little Boy Blue, come blow your horn.
The sheep's in the meadow,
The cow's in the corn.
Where is the boy who looks after the sheep?
He's under the haystack fast asleep.

Responsibility

What Is Responsibility?

Responsibility involves being trustworthy and dependable, being someone others can count on. Holding responsibility for something or someone means that we are answerable for our actions in that regard.

Why Is Responsibility Important? Things for Adults to Think About

■ Responsibility is more than just a character trait; it is an attitude that determines how we respond to everyday situations, many of which require some kind of moral decision. Are we responsible enough to keep our commitments, use our resources, employ tolerance and patience, be honest and fair, build our courage, show our cooperation and so forth? There are many ways to define responsibility and many ways to demonstrate it—being a responsible member of an organization, group or family; being responsible for our actions; being responsible for our belongings, pets and so on.

What does responsibility mean to you?

■ People are often irresponsible because they assume someone else will take up the slack. This happens in committees, in the office, in the family and in the classroom.

Think of situations where you have observed the pairing of an irresponsible person or persons with a responsible person or persons. Was the work load fair? Was the relationship fair?

■ When people are in a hurry, they often find it easier to do everything themselves as opposed to allowing others to assume some of the responsibility. Or it may be that they don't want to take the time to teach someone else what they need to do to help.

In our hurry-up society, it is becoming less likely that families will take time to teach children how to be responsible or to provide opportunities for them to practice being responsible.

Think about people you know. Do they usually delegate responsibility or do things themselves? Do they behave differently at work than at home? With friends than with family?

■ Part of responsibility requires making good choices. Making good choices means taking the time to evaluate your options. Children are often overwhelmed by having too many things to choose from—extra-curricular activities, toys, purchase options. When the choices are too many, most children will make no choice

at all. Children younger than seven make better and more defendable choices when they are given no more than three options.

How many gifts do children you know get for holidays, birthdays or special occasions? How many do they actually play with? How should extracurricular activities for children be handled?

■ Internally motivated people assume responsibility for what happens in their lives. When they are faced with a problem, they look inside themselves for solutions. They take responsibility for their lives. Externally motivated people look outside themselves and seek to shift blame to someone or something else.

Think about the traumas in life—lost job, divorce, financial loss, car accident, missed deadline. How can they be handled responsibly?

■ What happens when you are torn between two conflicting responsibilities? For example, when an important meeting at the office and your child's school play are scheduled on the same day and time.

What do you do in situations where there is conflict between your responsibilities and obligations? What happens when the conflict is between something you've planned for a long time and something a family member needs? Would you sacrifice your own needs for someone else's? Does responsibility require self-sacrifice? Is self-sacrifice healthy? What about responsibility to yourself?

■ Agrarian societies were dependent on large families sharing the responsibility of running the farm. Now that we no longer live in an agrarian society and technology has reduced our workloads, children go to school and come home to very few family responsibilities.

Can you think of ways to recreate that sense of responsibility in families today?

Talking With Children About Responsibility

Is responsibility a value worth keeping? Talk with children about the questions below and see what they think.

The Values Book

■ What does it mean to be responsible? Tell me what things you are responsible for.

■ Do you have responsibilities in your classroom? At home?

■ With young children, recite or sing "Little Boy Blue." Ask the children what Little Boy Blue was supposed to do. What was his job? Did he behave responsibly?

■ Do people have more or less responsibility when they are grown?

Develop children's language skills and continue the discussion of responsibility by weaving the following vocabulary words into your day.

accountable	dependable
actions	duties
answerable	judgment
choices	responsibility
chores	trustworthy

Things to Do in the Classroom

Activities for children of all ages

■ When children arrive at school, have them think about their day and draw a picture of the things they are going to accomplish.

Responsibility

■ Keep plants or pets in the classroom and make sure everyone shares in the responsibility of taking care of them. You might even want to schedule weekend care, assigning the responsibility to a different child each weekend.

■ Keep a helper chart in the room and rotate responsibility for classroom activities.

```
┌─────────────────────────────────┐
│                                 │
│      HELPER  CHART              │
│                                 │
│  Names        │    Job          │
│               │                 │
│  Dan          │  water plants   │
│  Erica        │  collect recycling│
│  Lucy         │   feed turtle   │
│  Pablo        │  clean paint jars│
│  Flora        │  lead song time │
│               │                 │
│               │                 │
│               │                 │
│               │                 │
└─────────────────────────────────┘
```

■ Play Who Stole the Cookie From the Cookie Jar.

Chorus	Who stole the cookie from the cookie jar?
	(Name) stole the cookie from the cookie jar.
(Name)	Who me?
Chorus	Yes, you!
(Name)	Not me.
Chorus	Then who?
(Name)	(New name) stole the cookie from the cookie jar.
	Repeat.

Talk about responsibility for our actions. Talk about blaming someone else.

■ Put on a class play or puppet show. Assign a responsibility to each child. After the performance, talk about how a successful production required everyone to be responsible for the work they were assigned. Being responsible means that others can count on you to do your part.

■ Discuss the responsibilities of your job with the children. Involve them in helping when possible (like taking the roll).

The Values Book

Activities for older children

■ Assign cooperative projects. For example, you might have groups of four children do a report on shadows. Assign each member of each group a responsibility. Have a recorder, a researcher, a materials monitor and a reporter.

■ Encourage children to brainstorm a list of ways they can assume responsibility for their school's appearance and image in the community. Invite children to decide if they want to assume the responsibilities they list and, if so, determine a way to share the work.

■ When children begin to play team sports, help them learn to play as a community. Team sports is an excellent way for children to internalize the concept of individual responsibilities contributing to the good of the whole. For example, in a soccer game the team may design a play, but that play won't come together unless all the individuals take responsibility for their assigned parts.

Working With Families: Ideas for Home

Activities for children of all ages

■ Take time to teach your children how to assume responsibility in family activities and then make sure you allow them to do their part.

■ Draw rebus pictures for children illustrating the items they need to bring home (sweater, lunch box, toy). Encourage them to check their list before leaving school to be sure all items are in their possession.

■ Use a responsibility chart to record family member responsibilities. Make sure you help your children see the contribution they make to family functioning. Be sure to increase responsibilities as children grow and mature.

Responsibilities	Mom	Dad	Alexis	Marissa	Dev
Set table					✔
Clear table				✔	
Put away clothes	✔	✔	✔	✔	✔
Make bed		✔	✔	✔	✔
Brush teeth	✔	✔	✔	✔	✔
Sweep floor			✔		
Load dishwasher			✔		
Take out garbage	✔				

The Values Book

■ Include pets and plants in your home. Involve your children in their care.

■ Model responsibility. If you are supposed to be somewhere—go. If you are a member of the civic club, be a responsible member. If you are given something to take care of—do it. Be responsible. As suggested in the chapter on commitment, if you start something, finish it.

■ Model responsibility to the greater community. For example, vote, give blood, take part in neighborhood meetings, participate in community service organizations.

■ Pay attention to what you say about your children and refrain from using labels. Children have a tendency to live up (or down) to our expectations. It's not uncommon to hear statements such as, "She's lazy just like her father" or "He's just as irresponsible as his brother." Statements like these can cause irreparable damage to both your children's self-esteem and your goal of promoting responsibility in your children.

Activities for older children

■ As children get older, involve them in family activities that require more responsibility like planning the menu for dinner or helping chart the route for a vacation.

■ When children are old enough to receive an allowance, help them learn how to save and spend wisely. Managing their money or being fiscally responsible will be a major part of their lives.

■ Teach children that their actions have consequences. If they forget materials or supplies they need for school, don't run to the store at night to get it for them. If they wait till the last minute to do a homework assignment, don't do the work for them, don't make excuses for them, and don't get them off the hook.

■ When children begin a project or take on a commitment, make sure they follow through. Don't sympathize with them because they've gotten bored with the idea or taken on more than they can handle. Responsible people finish what they start. By the same token, be sure to praise children when they go the extra mile.

■ Encourage children to play team sports. Make sure they see how their individual roles contribute to the overall success of the team. Observing the specific responsibilities of each player on a baseball team is a great way of seeing how each player contributes.

■ Participate in Take Your Child to Work programs. Involve your child in your daily responsibilities.

Books to Share With Children

Read books that illustrate and encourage responsibility. Check your library for some of those listed here. Each one provides opportunities to discuss the results of being answerable and accountable.

Can I Keep Him? by Steven Kellogg
Caring for My Baby Sister by Jane Moncure
Caring for My Home by Jane Moncure
Caring for My Things by Jane Moncure
Carl Goes to Day Care by Alexandra Day
City Green by Dyanne DiSalvo-Ryan
I Have a Pet by Shari Halpern
Music, Music for Everyone by Vera Williams
The Shepherd Boy by Kristine Franklin
Why Do Mosquitoes Buzz in People's Ears? by Verna Aardema

The Values Book

Tolerance

She had a peculiar name,
But she wasn't to blame.
She got it from her mother
Who's the same, same, same.
Catalina Magnalena Hootensteiner Bogantwiner
Hogan Logan Bogan was her name.

$\mathcal{T}$olerance

What Is Tolerance?

We practice tolerance when we

maintain a fair and objective

attitude toward others. People

often differ from us in opinion,

practice, belief or custom; toler-

ance allows us to accept and

appreciate our differences.

Why Is Tolerance Important? Things for Adults to Think About

■ During the sixties and the seventies, American society focused on individualism, on breaking away from established practices and beliefs, on "doing your own thing." In retrospect, that celebration of individualism may have provided fertile ground for growing feelings of superiority. Breaking off to go in another direction is often the result of believing another way is better. Sometimes we have strong emotional ties to our view. True tolerance is having your beliefs and respecting without judgment the beliefs of others even when they are different from your own.

Think of a characteristic or point of view you possess that you feel is "outside the box." Are you proud of that characteristic or point of view? What about others who may have a more traditional view or approach? How do you feel about their point of view?

■ Children's view of "the right way" is fixed in early adolescence. According to some experts, it is defined at age 12 and set by age 21. If children grow up with a limited view of possibilities, their definition of acceptable practices will be narrow.

How do you celebrate special holidays—Christmas, Hanukkah, New Year's Day, Kwanzaa—in your family? For example, if you celebrate Christmas do you open gifts on Christmas eve or Christmas morning? Do you have turkey or ham? Do you eat Christmas dinner at noon or in the evening?

Family times that are tied to traditions have a tendency to lock in one-right-way views. What will happen when children grow up and marry and are faced with the necessity of accommodating or integrating traditions that may be very different from those they have celebrated in the past?

■ Tolerance requires coping skills, especially when we are confronted by someone with conflicting values or points of view that have strong emotional overtones, such as politics and religion. In order to be tolerant, we must first keep our emotions in check.

When do you think people form their opinions about issues such as animal rights, welfare or the death penalty? What emotions might be involved? How might their opinions change over time?

■ Children are born without bias or prejudice. Their point of view and respect for other points of view will come from their family and society. Parents are the child's first teachers. Parents and teachers have a profound influence on children's attitudes and beliefs.

Examine your own biases and attitudes. Think of ways to consciously reduce any negative influence on the attitudes of the children around you.

■ The United States is, without question, a multicultural society. Most of us have daily contact with people of different races, genders, ages, religions and so on. Our stereotypes, prejudices and biases, both positive and negative, are constantly being challenged.

Do people categorize you based on their prejudices or stereotypes? Are they accurate? Can you be "generalized"? Have you ever been wrong about another person because you based your initial impression on a prejudice or stereotype?

■ Our individual behaviors encourage diversity and make life more interesting. Life would be boring if all our friends were just alike. We wouldn't have more than one political party if we all thought the same way. It's listening to other points of view that broadens our own.

Think of three or four of your friends. What things are unique to each one?

Talking With Children About Tolerance

Is tolerance a value worth keeping? Talk with children about the questions below and see what they think about tolerance.

■ Think about something that you do or believe in that is different from what your friends do or believe in. How does being different make you feel?

■ Has anyone ever made fun of you for being different? How did it make you feel?

Have you ever seen a friend making fun of another friend who was different in some way? What did you do?

■ Say the "Catalina Magnalena" poem with the children. Catalina's funny long name is a little different from most children's names. Talk about what an interesting name it is and how it makes Catalina different in a good and special way. We really are all very much alike though, aren't we—even while being, each one, unique?

■ Do you have a friend who is different? How is your friend different and what do you think about the differences? Can you think of ways you and your friend are alike?

Develop children's language skills and continue the discussion of tolerance by weaving the following vocabulary words into your day.

acceptance	fairness
beliefs	multicultural
customs	prejudice
conflict	tolerance
differences	understanding

Things to Do in the Classroom

Activities for children of all ages

■ Discuss the feelings of characters in stories that you read in the classroom. For example, how did the beast feel when the other animals ran away from him in *Who Is the Beast?* by Keith Baker.

■ When children have disagreements, help them identify their feelings and try to imagine the feelings of the other child. Tolerance begins by putting ourselves in the place of others.

Try a Peace Circle. Invite the two children involved in a disagreement to take turns explaining first their point of view and then their understanding of the other child's point of view. Allow each to suggest a resolution. The rest of the children can mediate if necessary. A Peace Circle allows everyone to profit by being involved in the process of resolving a disagreement.

■ Read a book that offers the opportunity to look at something from another perspective. For example, read *Two Bad Ants* by Chris Van Allsburg and discuss how different the kitchen looks from the ants' perspective. As a follow-up activity, invite children to explore the room with magnifying glasses and then draw a picture of the classroom from an ant's perspective.

✦✦✦✦✦✦ The Values Book

■ Incorporate classroom activities that focus on identifying similarities and differences. For example, ask how many children have a missing tooth, how many like grapefruit, how many speak more than one language, how many were born in September, how many are wearing red today.

■ During seasonal celebrations encourage children to describe the traditions they practice at home. Call attention to the multiplicity of ways to celebrate the same occasion and also the freedom of choice involved in whether one celebrates at all.

■ Provide variety in everything you do—snack foods, stories, methods of painting, field trips, classroom decorations and music. Encourage children to try new things and take on new roles. The more experiences children have, the broader their view of the world becomes.

■ Fill the classroom with materials that reflect diversity. For example, use posters that reflect variety in kinds of families and avoid stereotypes in gender-related jobs. Place a variety of ethnic dolls in the doll center. Choose books that reflect a balance in ethnic representation, authorship, gender roles and family configurations.

■ Have children change lunch partners occasionally. This provides opportunities for them to experience many different personalities and maybe even customs.

■ Keep a chart of story characters. How many main characters are male? Female? How many are people of color? How many are physically challenged? How many represent any minority? Talk about your findings at the end of a week or month. What do the children notice?

STORY CHARACTERS				Other distinguishing characteristics
Story	Main character	Male	Female	
Amazing Grace	Grace		✓	African American
The Last Dragon	Peter	✓		Asian-American
Daisy's Garden	Daisy		✓	
Annie and the Wild Animals	Annie		✓	

■ Choose a familiar folktale and read versions of it from different cultures. For example, Little Red Riding Hood is also known as Lon Po Po; the Gingerbread Boy is Der Lebkuchenman, Johnny Cake and the Little Cookie. Talk about the similarities and differences among the different versions of the story. The children's librarian at your local library can help you locate stories.

Activities for older children

■ Solicit pen pals from another country. Help children identify similarities and differences in customs.

■ Play a familiar game several different ways, such as jacks, hopscotch or mankala. You'll find several ideas in books such as *Hopscotch Around the World* and *Jacks Around the World* by Mary Lankford. Discuss the fun diversity adds to the activity.

■ Before playing competitive games, help children understand the sportsmanship associated with losing. Discuss games as one of many activities that are often more fun in the middle than before or after. Learning to lose is part of tolerance.

Working With Families: Ideas for Home

Activities for children of all ages

■ Lead your child to understand that diversity provides us with more interesting lives. Talk about ways you and your family have already incorporated aspects of other cultures into your life. What different foods do you eat? How many kinds of music do you enjoy? What about your clothes? Your vocabulary? What other kinds of things have you learned or borrowed from different cultures?

■ Provide opportunities for children to interact with a diverse group of other children. It might be a good idea to sign up for dance classes or gymnastic activities in an area of town where the ethnic mix of people is different from the area in which you live.

■ Travel as much as possible and use the opportunity to help children notice similarities and differences of geographic regions. Keep discussions free of bias.

■ Watch television with your children. Help them identify racial, ethnic and other stereotypical situations in commercials and in programs. There are plenty.

■ Be a good role model. As children are introduced to your values and traditions, make them aware that other people may have values and traditions that are different but not wrong. Avoid judgment statements about weight, gender, religious tenets, skin color or clothing that make characteristics of others seem less desirable

■ Research the origin of your child's name. Was it passed down through your family or is your child the first person in the family to have the name? You may be surprised at the cultural origin.

■ Let your children see you taking part in activities that are outside traditional gender roles. For example, males might take care of the baby or cook. Females might wash the car or use power tools. Encourage your children to think outside traditional gender roles.

Activities for older children

■ Provide opportunities for children to be involved in activities that protect the rights of others, such as animal rights, children's rights or senior citizens' rights.

■ Be honest. When you expose one of your biases or prejudices, acknowledge its existence and discuss it with your children.

Books to Share With Children

Read books that illustrate and encourage tolerance. Check your library for some of those listed here. Each one provides opportunities to discuss the results of being open to others.

All the Colors We Are by Katie Kissinger
Chester's Way by Kevin Henkes
The Garden of Happiness by Erika Tamar
Margaret and Margarita by Lynn Reiser
Mrs. Katz and Tush by Patricia Polacco
My Best Friend by Mignon Hinds
New Friends, True Friends, Stuck-Like-Glue Friends by Virginia Kroll
Old Henry by Joan Blos
The Paper Bag Princess by Robert Munsch
Sing a Song of People by Lois Lenski
The Sneetches and Other Stories by Dr. Seuss
This Is Our House by Michael Rosen
This Is the Way We Go to School by Edith Baer
Whoever You Are by Mem Fox
Who Is the Beast? by Keith Baker
Who's in a Family? by Robert Skutch

Index

A

B

C

Suggested books

A

ABC I Like Me   88
by Nancy Carlson
Alejandro's Gift   133
by Richard Albert
Alexander and the Terrible, Horrible,
    No Good, Very Bad Day   16, 133
by Judith Viorst
Alfie Gives a Hand   16
by Shirley Hughes
All by Myself   35, 88
by Anna Grossnickle Hines
All Stuck Up   124
by Linda Hayward
All the Colors We Are   154
by Katie Kissinger
Amazing Grace   16, 46
by Mary Hoffman
Amos and Boris   63, 95
by William Steig
Angus and the Cat   46
by Marjorie Flack

E, F

G

H

I

T

U, V, W

Y